CAMBRIDGE LIBRARY COLLECTION

Books of enduring scholarly value

Slavery and Abolition

The books reissued in this series include accounts of historical events and movements by eye-witnesses and contemporaries, as well as landmark studies that assembled significant source materials or developed new historiographical methods. The series includes work in social, political and military history on a wide range of periods and regions, giving modern scholars ready access to influential publications of the past.

The Trials of the Slave Traders, Samuel Samo, Joseph Peters, and William Tufft

In 1812 a number of slave traders were prosecuted in Sierra Leone, the focus of Britain's efforts to eradicate the trade. First published in 1813, this report is believed to have been written by the presiding judge, Robert Thorpe. The trials provoked debate as Thorpe found one trader guilty, but commuted his sentence on the condition that other traders were persuaded to cease their business. Another was dealt with severely as he displayed complicity in evading the laws. Thorpe's judgments relied upon not only the application of the anti-slavery laws, but also the notion of natural laws transcending those of nations, a notion which came under consideration in the landmark *Somerset v. Stewart* case of 1772, concerning an escaped slave. Published in 1876, a report on this case is also reissued here. Taken together, these two texts provide valuable source material on the history of the slave trade's abolition.

Cambridge University Press has long been a pioneer in the reissuing of out-of-print titles from its own backlist, producing digital reprints of books that are still sought after by scholars and students but could not be reprinted economically using traditional technology. The Cambridge Library Collection extends this activity to a wider range of books which are still of importance to researchers and professionals, either for the source material they contain, or as landmarks in the history of their academic discipline.

Drawing from the world-renowned collections in the Cambridge University Library and other partner libraries, and guided by the advice of experts in each subject area, Cambridge University Press is using state-of-the-art scanning machines in its own Printing House to capture the content of each book selected for inclusion. The files are processed to give a consistently clear, crisp image, and the books finished to the high quality standard for which the Press is recognised around the world. The latest print-on-demand technology ensures that the books will remain available indefinitely, and that orders for single or multiple copies can quickly be supplied.

The Cambridge Library Collection brings back to life books of enduring scholarly value (including out-of-copyright works originally issued by other publishers) across a wide range of disciplines in the humanities and social sciences and in science and technology.

The Trials of the Slave Traders, Samuel Samo, Joseph Peters, and William Tufft

And *The Fugitive Slave Circulars*

ANONYMOUS

CAMBRIDGE
UNIVERSITY PRESS

CAMBRIDGE
UNIVERSITY PRESS

University Printing House, Cambridge, CB2 8BS, United Kingdom

Cambridge University Press is part of the University of Cambridge.

It furthers the University's mission by disseminating knowledge in the pursuit of
education, learning and research at the highest international levels of excellence.

www.cambridge.org
Information on this title: www.cambridge.org/9781108078740

© in this compilation Cambridge University Press 2015

This edition first published 1813
This digitally printed version 2015

ISBN 978-1-108-07874-0 Paperback

THE

TRIALS

OF THE

SLAVE TRADERS,

AT SIERRA LEONE,

In April and June,

1812.

THE

TRIALS

OF THE

SLAVE TRADERS,

SAMUEL SAMO, JOSEPH PETERS,

AND

WILLIAM TUFFT,

TRIED

IN APRIL AND JUNE, 1812,

BEFORE THE

HON. ROBERT THORPE, L.L.D.

Chief Justice of Sierra Leone, &c. &c.

WITH

TWO LETTERS ON THE SLAVE TRADE,

FROM A GENTLEMAN RESIDENT AT SIERRA LEONE TO AN ADVOCATE
FOR THE ABOLITION, IN LONDON.

———

LONDON:

PRINTED FOR SHERWOOD, NEELEY, AND JONES,
PATERNOSTER-ROW; AND TO BE HAD OF
ALL OTHER BOOKSELLERS.

———

1813.

James Gillet, Printer, Crown court, Fleet-street, London.

INTRODUCTION.

THE leading motive for publishing the Trials
of the Slave Traders is, to afford the British Legislature, the Government, and the people in general, an early and correct view of the operation
of the recent slave felony act of parliament: an act
which reflects the highest honour on those whose
humanity was so determined and conspicuous in
conducting to a happy issue the long and strenu-
ously contested question of African emancipation.

It is due to those great, good, and eloquent men
who, with unshaken perseverance, exerted themselves in this truly benevolent cause, that they
should be made acquainted, at the earliest possible
moment, with the beneficial effects arising from
their disinterested zeal in behalf of those thousands
of enslaved Africans who could do nothing for
themselves.

The characters engaged in bringing about this
new and humane system might easily be named;
but they are so well known, that no fresh
publicity could add to their honour, or enlarge
their celebrity, which are already complete; and
the consciousness of their just and wise intentions
is a reward so ample, as to preclude their deriving

B

any acquisition of gratification from express personal approbation. The world will always remember, and often mention, them ; and it is impossible they can be forgotten by historians; for when they speak of the British legislative acts of the nineteenth century, they must dwell with delight and enthusiasm in honest praise of the names of those who contended with unrivalled eloquence, unanswerable arguments, and final success, against slavery. Besides, the reporter of these Trials, and the author of this Introduction, having no object to attain, except extending the cause of humanity, would preserve himself free from even the suspicion of adulation.

It will be found, from a perusal of these Trials, and a consideration of the country inhabited by the slave-trading delinquents, that a death-blow has been struck at that execrable traffic, throughout a great extent of the western coast of Africa.

Discovery will also be made, that notwithstanding a very short interval only has elapsed since the wisdom of parliament declared that trading in slaves should be a felony, yet the act thus declaratory has already been brought into effective and full operation, by those intrusted by the government with the important power of administering the laws of Great Britain, in a distant part of her vast dominions.

The cruelty and turpitude practised by the slave traders will also appear, and serve to add an increased horror towards that diabolical commerce,

at the mere contemplation of which, every mind
not hardened by the profits accruing from it involuntarily shudders. The facts here developed
cannot fail to originate many important reflections.
The legislator will consider whether something
is not still necessary to be done, though he
may exultingly own much has been achieved in
behalf of the poor African. He will consider
whether the energy of this nation, foremost in
power and knowledge beyond all others on earth,
cannot render more perfect that system of African
melioration, which it hath already attempted with
such signal success.

The executive government will congratulate
themselves that one of the most benignant laws
which it is their glory and their happiness to be
instrumental in dispensing, hath been promptly
acted upon in the best possible manner (where
discretion is allowed) by those to whose charge
they are committed abroad; and the people of
England will feel a glow of sincere and unmingled
delight, that though they live in a day of war un-
paralleled in extent against them, a war waged by
the slaves of almost all nations, who for them are
striving to forge fetters, while they are kindly
breaking the bolts which bind, and loosening the
chains that torture, their fellow-creatures in the
distant climes of Africa.

The Letters which follow the Trials will be
found to contain many facts and opinions, and to
treat on subjects relative to the slave-trade which

have not been hitherto well known, or much considered.

These Trials were reported by a gentleman at Sierra Leone, who was present during their progress, and who was personally engaged in measures for effecting the abolition. He sent them to his correspondent in London, who now submits them to the public ; and he feels no hesitation in assuring himself, that at this juncture they could receive nothing better calculated to meet and gratify both their hearts and their understandings

THE TRIAL

OF

SAMUEL SAMO,

SLAVE TRADER,

Indicted for trading in Slaves, and tried at the
Court of Oyer and Terminer, held in SIERRA
LEONE, on the Coast of Africa, before the
Honourable Chief Justice THORPE, L. L. D.
on the 7th, 8th, 9th, and 10th of April, 1812.

THE Court met on the 7th of April, James Becket, Esq.
the clerk, having sworn the Grand Jury; the Chief Justice
then charged them, in a most impressive manner, on their
various duties, and concluded in these words:

GENTLEMEN,

The calendar furnishes one crime more,
on which it is necessary to instruct you, but its novelty
and importance will oblige me to be minutely explicit.

Indictments will be laid before you against Samuel Samo
and Charles Hickson for trading in slaves, since the first
of September, 1811, in violation of the fifty-first of the
King, chap. 23. The British parliament passed above
ten bills for meliorating the condition, affording comfort,
and preventing the cruelties that had been practised on
the negroes in their transatlantic passage. They were

acts of great benevolence; but the wealth and party influence of those fed by the negroes' unrewarded labour, was so commanding, that the Abolition Act could not be passed until that great statesman, Mr. Fox (carrying his purity of principle and consistent integrity into place and power,) effected it by the assistance of government. Forfeitures and confiscations were found inadequate for abolition; and the same philanthropy continuing to illumine the British senate, an act constituting the slave trade felony was passed, to render former acts more effective, and the abolition complete. The first time of making this valuable act operative has devolved on you; the principles of British jurisprudence will not tolerate slavery; liberty does not depend on complexion; it is dispensed, it is secured by law, in the administration of which, distinction of person is not acknowledged. Even in the days of Queen Elizabeth, it was emphatically said, " the air of a British government was too pure for a slave to breathe." It has been said to me by one, that " this cargo of slaves is the property of such an individual, or these slaves are national property." I know of no property in humanity, nor of any law, divine or human, that bestows it! Man, formed after the image of God, created and made by his ordinance, is the property of God, and his only! Another has audaciously said to me, " these blacks are only fitted for slavery." I have answered, " suppose you were in a kingdom of blacks, where some white man might be chained to an oak, or toiling in a fort, and to your plea for his liberation, it was replied, these white fellows are only fitted for such servitude. How much philanthropy or philosophy would you allow this contained? Yet there it might be only individual calamity fortuitously entailed, while here we have national misery systematically established!

This act is uncommonly strong and wide in its reach, [here the learned Judge read the greatest part of the first clause.] Thus any person trading in any way in slaves, or aiding or abetting such traffic in any way, is considered a felon, and punished with fourteen years transportation, or to be kept at hard labour for five years; now these slave-factors are degraded to pickpockets and swindlers. But should this infernal commerce be continued; if mercenary miscreants can be found, whom fines, forfeitures, and infamy, cannot controul, whom no principle of morality, liberty, justice, humanity, or policy, can restrain, but that innumerable cruelties, multifarious casualties, and premature deaths, are still continued to be heaped on the unoffending sons of Africa; if those innocent human beings are still to be torn from their country, their habitations, their parents, children, and friends, for the miserable gratification of a little rum and tobacco; then I have no doubt the Almighty will continue the enlightened benevolence of England, and that an act will pass the British legislature, considering the monsters what they really are, *hostes humani generis,* (much worse than pirates,) and authorize their being put to death wherever found, or to what nation soever they may belong; and even after this, they should be thankful that the law of England does not allow torture to be inflicted; for if the law of retaliation were let loose on them, their sufferings would be excessive and constant. It is the very essence of justice to apportion punishment to offence; and could the cargoes of slaves we have constantly exhibited in this colony, could the animated skeletons that are landed here, imploring death for relief, be visible in England, an universal exclamation would involuntarily burst from that inestimable people —" Without ocular demonstration, we could not have believed that human depravity could have extended to these enormities—extirpate these monsters !"

Gentlemen, you have a great duty to perform; England will look to you for its discharge; the happiness of thousands will rest upon it. I know the prisoners are personally known to many of you; but I have tried your integrity, and am confident—Remember your oath, that you will diligently inquire, and true presentment make; calmly and dispassionately compare the statute and the indictment, and, if the proofs will warrant the accusation, send it for investigation before the Court and a jury, by finding the bills.

The Grand Jury found true bills of indictment against Samuel Samo and Charles Hickson.

On Samo's being put to the bar, and the indictment being read, Mr. M******, as counsel for the prisoner, applied to the Court for leave to shew that the prisoners could not be tried, as indicted under the 51st of George the Third, chapter 23, that statute attaching only to British subjects, and that Mr. Samuel Samo was a Dutchman. He took strong ground, and was replied to by James Biggs, Esq., who was appointed to act as Attorney-general for the colony, and who proved that Samo had resided sixteen years in the Rio Pongas, considered himself as an Englishman, and claimed British protection; that he only claimed the privilege of a Dutchman when he dreaded the effects of the Abolition acts; and that the place of his birth was not proved, and only a short residence at Surinam established.

The Court over-ruled the objection, and the trial proceeded. The Petit Jury before whom this case was tried consisted of the following gentlemen, who were accordingly sworn:

Jas. Willie, Esq. Foreman,	Mr. William Taylor,
Kenneth M'Cawley, Esq.	Mr. Scipio Lucas,
Mr. John Bowles,	Mr. James Reid,
Mr. George Warren,	Mr. Hector Peters,
Mr. Peter Kennedy,	Mr. Robert Robertson,
Mr. John M'Cawley,	Mr. J. M'Cawley Wilson.

The Court was very much crowded: the novelty of the case produced a general and lively interest. Mr. Samo, on his arraignment, seemed deeply affected; he pleaded Not Guilty.

Mr. Biggs stated the case on the part of the Crown.

My Lord, and Gentlemen of the Jury, This is an indictment against Samuel Samo for feloniously dealing in slaves, in direct violation of an act of parliament passed in the fifty-first year of the reign of his present Majesty, for the more effectually abolishing the slave trade. The cause is, indeed, one of the most important, both in itself and its consequences, that hath occupied the public attention at any period in the nineteenth century. It is not merely the interests of an individual, a village, a city, a country, or a single kingdom, which this case is calculated to effect; but it embraces the essential concerns of one quarter of the globe we inhabit, and involves the security and morals, the happiness and liberty, of millions yet to live. Under circumstances of this vast magnitude, my Lord, and Gentlemen of the Jury, I feel confident, however deficient I may be in eloquence, your indulgence and your duty will afford me a patient hearing throughout the laborious investigation into which I shall be obliged to enter. In a cause to be tried before a Court so high and learned, and a jury and audience so respectable, I could wish, for the renown of this case, that the prosecution of it had fallen into the hands of some one of those eminent luminaries of the British bar, who are highly distinguished for eloquence to persuade and knowledge to convince. But, since the task has devolved on me, I shall endeavour to make up for fluency by zeal, and for oratory by fact. My Lord, and Gentlemen of the Jury, a combination of fortunate and singular circumstances has put me in possession of events and information relative to the

c

slave trade in general, and of this case in particular, which I am enabled to substantiate by legal evidence, and removes a large share of the diffidence which I must otherwise have experienced in appearing before you this day.

I would take this occasion to remark, that the humane and anxious desire of the Parliament of the British empire to abolish the barbarous traffic in slaves is universally known; the remotest tribe on the face of the earth are apprized long ere this of the benevolent desire of every good mind in England, that, however savage might be the race of distant climes, their land should not contain a single slave. This feeling, the first-born of an admirable constitution, did not content itself with mere latent existence, but was openly manifested by treaties, negotiations, missions, and many other public acts, done and published from time to time during the present reign. Of late years we find, with undivided satisfaction, that though the unwise and tyrannical system of Dutch, Portuguese, Danish, Spanish, and French colonization, England was obliged, unwillingly, to acquiesce in the temporary policy of an iniquitous slave trade, yet she never for a moment lost sight of the grand and ultimate determination of effecting its radical and signal prostration. Evidence of this assertion clearly appears in the well-directed acts of parliament enjoining benevolent restrictions on all vessels and all persons concerned in slave trading.

Gentlemen of the Jury, you will allow me to bring to your thoughts the leading features of your indispensable duty; you have often been called upon as arbiters of the life, liberty, honour, and property of your fellow-subject. You are now called upon to protect the honour and dignity of your King, and to support those laws which, under his virtue and authority, were enacted for the deliverance of this country from the wretchedness of slavery.

It will appear to you by the evidence which I shall produce, that the prisoner at the bar has held those laws and their authority in contempt, and has violated them in defiance of warning and knowledge. You should, therefore, as good subjects and conscientious men, be careful to suffer no undue partiality, no warmth of friendship, if any you formerly possessed for the accused, to give the impulse of feeling a predominance over your better judgments, which can end only in betraying you from the strict line of your duty and your patriotism. The penalties of the act under which the prisoner at the bar now stands accused are, it is solemnly true, long, severe, and ignominious; so it was necessary and just they should be; but if the prisoner hath incurred them, it will be your imperative duty, as faithful jurors, to visit them upon him, by a verdict of Guilty, notwithstanding you may sympathize with him as fellow-men; but that would be a false compassion, which saves one at the probable sacrifice of thousands. That the cause of Samuel Samo now arraigned is one of great novelty and intricacy must be confessed. It is novel, because it is the first ever tried under the Slave Felony Act; it is intricate, because cunning art and contrivance have been employed to screen the violators of the law from the piercing eye of offended justice. The novelty will cease by the success of that vigilance which is now exerting to bring to light and legal investigation the concealed instruments of the slave trade; and the intricacy of the present case, I believe, I shall be able to unravel to the satisfaction of your Lordship, and the conviction of the Jury.

The evidence now to be produced will discover a system, by which the men who carry on the slave trade hope to obtain the profits of a base and barbarous traffic, and yet escape the just punishment which they ought to suffer for their crimes; and it will also shew that Samuel Samo, as charged in the five counts in the indictment, did ship off from the coast of Africa as principal, and also as aider and abettor, a certain number of slaves, in the months of August, September, October, and November, 1811; and that he shipped from the Rio Pongas, slaves, in the months of December, 1811, and January, 1812. I shall adduce clear proof that the prisoner did ship off from the coast of Africa between 30 and 40 persons, to be bought, sold, and dealt with, and transhipped as slaves, and that, therefore, you ought to bring in against him a verdict of Guilty.

Here began the evidence on the part of the Crown.

[To condense the trial as much as possible, the substance of the evidence only will be given, without detailing the whole of the questions and answers.]

THOMAS CURTIS sworn.

Evidence.—He has resided in the Rio Pongas a long time: he knew that Samuel Samo sent off slaves from the Rio Pongas some time in January, 1812; the master of the vessel in which the slaves went, bartered with one Wilson for the cargo; the goods for purchasing the cargo of slaves were landed at Wilson's factory; the vessel carried off 120 slaves; he heard, and believes, that Samuel Samo, Mr. John Ormond, Mr. Stiles Lightburn, Mr. J. Faber, and William Cunningham Wilson, freighted the vessel off with slaves; he knew the vessel called the Eagle under Spanish colours; she arrived in the Rio Pongas in September, 1811. The master of the Eagle bartered for 120 slaves; they were procured from Samo (the prisoner), Ormond, William Laurence, Thomas Curtis (the witness), Lightburn, and Faber. Samo supplied 25 slaves; the factors made an agreement to supply the cargo of slaves among them to get the vessel off quickly; there was tobacco, gunpowder, cloth, and rum, paid for the slaves.

Cross-examined by Mr. H*****s.

He is not in Mr. Samo's employ, but in the employ of witness's father; he heard Wilson say, that Samo was to send him slaves for the vessel, and saw the barter to be paid for them; he did not see Samo send the slaves to Wilson; he thinks the Samadada another name for the Eagle; he heard Mr. Wilson say that Samo sent off slaves in that cargo; he heard the natives of the Soosoo country say, Samo sent off 20 slaves in January, 1812; he heard and believes that Samo sent off slaves in the vessel also that sailed in September, 1811. The natives told him he had; the natives always inform the factors who supply the cargoes of slaves for each vessel, but the factors do not inform each other.

Philip Gordon *sworn.*

Evidence.—The schooner Eagle came into the Rio Pongas in October, 1811, and went off with a cargo of slaves; Samuel Samo, the prisoner, shipped off ten slaves; Samo's cooper told him that he had got tobacco and rum for the slaves from Wilson: he saw the slaves come from Samo's factory, and saw Samo's people take them on board the vessel in his canoes; he saw slaves in Samo's factory in irons eight weeks ago.

Cross-examined.

Evidence—He saw slaves on board the Eagle; he knows Samo's slaves and people; the supercargo told witness they were Samo's slaves; the vessel sailed off in November, 1811; he saw the slaves come off from Samo's wharf in Samo's canoes; Samo's people, and the master of Samo's vessel, said the slaves were from Samo's factory; he saw the vessel over the Rio Pongas bar, with all sail set; he went over the bar with her; Mr. Samo's clerk told him Mr. Samo had purchased the slaves.

James Cooper *sworn.*

Evidence —He is a cooper by trade, and coopered the casks for the vessel; he saw Mr. Samo make a bargain with Mr. Wilson for slaves; Wilson gave Samo rum, tobacco, and gunpowder, for the slaves; he opened a cask by Mr. Wilson's order, for Samo to look at the articles; he saw the ten slaves Samo sent off, he saw them on board the vessel, he saw the vessel sail off with them, the vessel had previously landed her cargo at Wilson's factory; the factors made up the cargo of slaves among them; there were about 150 slaves; witness saw no dollars or ivory for barter of slaves, but there was tobacco and rum; Mr. Samo took his own share of the pay for the slaves to his factory.

Cross-examined.

Evidence.—He is not a slave; he was in the river when the slave vessel sailed; he lived with Mr. Lawrance; Wilson sent for him to cooper the casks; he saw no money paid for goods that Samo received; he saw Mr. Samo take the goods away; he saw Samo's slaves on board; Samo's people told witness that they were his slaves; he was three weeks on board himself, he asked the people who brought the slaves, where they came from, and they told him, from Samo's factory; the slaves came in a canoe; he saw them come along side the schooner, at Wilson's factory, and saw them put on board the schooner; there were ten slaves; when he saw the slaves they were far from Samo's factory.

Malcolm Brodie *sworn.*

Evidence.—The last slave vessel he saw leave the Rio Pongas, was in January, 1812; he does not know of Mr. Samo supplying any slaves; the slave dealers trade as secretly as possible, to evade the acts.

Wm. Skelton *sworn.*

Evidence.—He was born in the Rio Pongas, is 18 years old, and was educated at Liverpool, in England; he is two years returned from England; he is clerk to Samo, the prisoner, who was a slave-factor, in the Rio Pongas, but has left that river, and settled at the Isles de Loss; Mr. Samo sent off the last slaves in January, 1812. The slaves were fifteen in number; he thinks he sent them on freight to the Havannah; Mr. Samo's correspondent there is Colin Mitchell. Caruth was the name of the super-cargo of the vessel in which Mr. Samo shipped off the slaves; Mr. Samo sent two boys away on wages, he sent the fifteen slaves away in the name of the witness, Wm. Skelton; he heard, and believes, Mr. Samo had a share in the cargo of slaves that went off in November, 1811; and that he sent off at that time twenty slaves, and half a ton of rice. There were goods came from Wilson's to Samo's factory at that time, consisting of two hogsheads of tobacco, gunpowder, cloth, rum, and molasses; witness supposes these articles might have been the price of the twenty slaves; he believes the vessel landed her cargo of goods for the barter of slaves at Wilson's factory. Mr. Samo has now at his factory between twenty and thirty new slaves, who have been let out of irons above two months by the witness himself. He never heard Mr. Samo say he was an Englishman.

A letter was here produced from Wilson to Samo.

Wilson's hand-writing was proved, and it was also proved that it was taken out of Samo's private desk. Wilson acknowledges in this letter that he had sent two slaves of Samo by the vessel Samadada, or Eagle, and accounts with Samo for them. A letter from the prisoner to Wm. Skelton was proved, which informed him that Samo was still in prison, that he was doubtful and apprehensive what might be his fate. He charged the witness to take care of his writing desks, and papers; not to have any communication with Mr. James Biggs, who was collecting evidence in the Rio Pongas; not to make direct answers to any questions that might be put; to keep out of the way of being questioned; to conceal the prisoner's papers; and that for his fidelity he should be doubly rewarded. Another paper was produced from Samo's desk, shewing that a combination was entered into by the principal factors in the Rio Pongas, not to have any dealings with the blacks and native traders under a forfeiture of 500 bars or dollars, the object of this agreement was to monopolize the slave trade to themselves; this was signed by Cunningham Wilson, Samuel Samo, Charles Hickson, W. Leigh, and John Ormond, dated the 25th of November, 1809; the signatures were proved.

A bill of lading was produced from Samo's desk, acknowledged to be in the hand-writing of the witness, who drew the bill by the direction of Samo, stating that fifteen slaves are to be delivered in good condition at the Havannah, dated the 12th of January, 1812. It appeared from the bill of lading that the slaves were all branded on the right thigh; the witness being asked, how the brand was effected, replied, that it was done with a hot pipe, which burned the mark on the flesh. The witness had received no compensation from Mr. Samo for these services; he does not know whether Samo is a Dutchman or not, but heard he had written for a certificate of the place of his nativity, and has heard him speak of brothers in Holland.

Cross-examination.

Evidence.—Witness thought Samo wished to give up the slave trade; he heard Mr. Samo speak of being a Dutchman in May, 1810.

The evidence for the crown being closed, Mr. H*****s, assistant counsel with Mr. H******n, rose and stated to the Court that it had been his wish not to have any thing to do in this cause; but as he had been assigned to defend the prisoner in the absense of the leading counsel who was sick, he would endeavour to shew that the prisoner was by no means so criminal as the attorney-general had attempted to prove; and he now begged the Court to consider the respectability of the prisoner, and the good name that would be given him by respectable persons to be called forward, and that he was at the point of renouncing the slave trade at the time he was apprehended. The prisoner had left the Rio Pongas, and had settled at the Isles de Loss. These, and several other well adapted observations, were made by Mr. H*****s,* who discovered much ability in behalf of the prisoner; he prayed permission of the Court to read a paper, which the prisoner had handed him, which ran thus: " I was born at Amsterdam, in the year 1770; and left there for the colony of Surinam, in the year 1788, where I arrived, and staid until the year 1795; I then went to North America, made two voyages there and back, and from thence came out to Africa, in the beginning of 1797, where I have since been, of which I was upwards of 14 years in the Rio Pongas, and of course out of the British jurisdiction. Now I have to ask whether a man under those cirumstances ought to be amenable to British laws? or can be considered a British subject? I do not only declare that I am innocent of the charge laid against me, but that I have, for a considerable time, been doing all in my power toward the grand object, the total

---

* The Editor applied to the prisoner's counsel for their notes, but could not procure them; the substance of the defence is given, with their acknowledgment and consent; their names are not given, probably because they would not like the world to know they had defended slave traders.

abolition of the slave trade, by withdrawing from the Rio Pongas, and now establishing myself in the Isles de Loss, where I have the promise of a good piece of land, and (if it please the Almighty) I will convince the inhabitants and natives of Africa what can be done in respect to agriculture in this country. After all, I am not conscious how a man should be amenable to laws from which he can reap no benefit whatsoever, as these laws are made for British subjects only. Now, was I to go to England, and there solicit for any pecuniary office, or attempt to purchase lands, I suppose I should have to prove myself an Englishman, (which all the world cannot do), or I cannot obtain either." Mr. H*****s hoped, if the prisoner was found guilty, that the clemency of the Court would shew him all the mercy the act allowed to their discretion. The prisoner having ended his statement,

Mr. GEORGE NICOL *was sworn.*

He had known Mr. Samo a long time; he was a very quiet man, one of the best of the factors in the Rio Pongas.

Mr. ALEXANDER SMITH *sworn.*

He had known Mr. Samo a long time; that he knew nothing bad of him but his dealing in slaves; he never was one of the active bad hands in the Rio Pongas.

Mr. M'MILLAR *sworn.*

Setting aside dealing in slaves, he believed Mr. Samo was a good man; he was always a very quiet man, and never engaged in any of the riots in the Rio Pongas.

[Here closed the evidence in favour of the prisoner.]

Mr. Biggs, the counsel for the crown, rose in reply, and, requesting the indulgence of the Court, proceeded thus:

My Lord, and Gentlemen of the Jury,

Though in this case I confidently anticipated the result of the evidence, yet that result has been the anticipation of truth ; it fully appears that every count in the indictment is supported by evidence that can neither be questioned or refuted. I am indebted to your Lordship and the Jury for your attention in this long investigation ; and submit whether this be not a proper occasion to state by what means this body of unexpected evidence has burst upon us, and developed the continuance and mode of pursuing the slave commerce practised by the remaining slave factors.

The daring violations against the acts of parliament prohibiting the traffic in slaves, which were known to be daily committed in the Rio Pongas by British subjects, could not fail to attract the attention of the government of this colony; when these violations had, in the hope of impunity, attained a gross pitch of criminality, no longer to be tolerated, the prisoner at the bar, and one of his slaving associates, were apprehended and secured; it was not certain that the evidence then had would absolutely establish their guilt ; to obviate this difficulty, his Excellency the Governor and my Lord the Chief Justice devised a plan, highly to their honour and fame, of obtaining the essential proof from the place where these illegalities had been committed. This plan was to send to the King of the Soosoo nation for such persons as were qualified to be evidences for the crown ; and I congratulate myself that it was appointed to me to bring them forth. It was proposed to me to present myself to Mungo Catty, King of the Soosoo nation, and, with his permission, bring away such residents in his dominions as I might think proper, pursuant to written instructions from his Excellency Governor Maxwell. This I did, and the evidence you have this day heard is the fruits of the attempt. I request your Lordship and Gentlemen of the Jury to listen to a few observations respecting the gentlemen whom I brought from various parts of the Rio Pongas. In coming to this colony, these gentlemen have been put to some expense and much inconvenience; they have fulfilled their parts as evidences for the crown; it would be unjust in me to withhold the public expression of my entire satisfaction of their conduct. I promised the King under whom they lived that they should be protected, and when the trials were over, that they should be safely restored to their former places of abode. Of Mr. William Skelton I ought to speak in particular; he and the other gentlemen have not shewn a little virtue in coming forward; but Mr. Skelton is celtainly in a peculiar manner distinguished. He was a long time balanced between a wish to be true to his former friend and master, and his desire of rendering his duty to the country in which he was educated and protected. When I had convinced him of the exceeding wickedness and cruelty of the slave trade, and of the humanity of putting an end to it, he no longer hesitated, or thought it incumbent on him to hold confidence with him who was at the head of the infamous traffic, but yielded at once to a spontaneous and candid avowal. I trust that the remunerative liberality of the Government will not overlook the worth and the services of this young man. To his behaviour there is a striking contrast in the conduct of some of the slave traders, who refused to renounce the monstrous traffic, and who still remain in the Rio Pongas. I allude to John Ormond, Robert Cunningham Wilson, and J. Faber; but I will not enlarge on the subject. Justice will overtake them. I cannot close without lamenting the death of one of the principal witnesses, who first gave the information, and who was to have been heard this day : but " who can tell what a day may bring forth?" Mr. David James Lawrence fell a victim to disease and a broken heart, in consequence of the vile treatment and persecution of the slave traders, who hated him because he had renounced their fellowship and business, and complied with the laws of his country. Had this gentleman lived, he would have given such testimony as would have put it beyond all doubt, whether this very town was not the heart from which all the arteries and the veins of the slave trading system has for years been animated and supplied; he would have proved that the poison which the British Government wished to counteract in Africa, is in a large proportion compounded by persons in England who profess in public, under the hypocritical garb of religion, that they desire only to complete the abolition. But, to return to the evidence, I conceive, my Lord, and Gentlemen of the Jury, the proofs produced are perfectly conclusive, and that nothing short of a verdict of Guilty can discharge the duty of the Jury; nor can I see that the prisoner can expect it otherwise. How can he expect that this Jury will, to the detriment of their country, and the violation of their consciences, extend that mercy to him which the prisoner has so often denied to hundreds (perhaps thousands) of his fellow-creatures, for such were the slaves he has shipped off for years, however black their skins, ignorant their minds, or unprotected their condition. Consider, Gentlemen of the Jury, that merciful Providence, that has watched over you, and guarded you from being chained as a slave in the slave-yard of Charleston Factory.* Why should the white man be entitled to bind the black man's wrists or ancles with the ignominious badge of slavery? Viewing mankind from the North Pole to the South, it is discovered, that in various climates there are various hues of complexion, from the most

---

* Charleston Factory is the name of Samo's slave establishment, in Rio Pongas.

brilliant and lovely white, with equally delicate limb and feature, to the permanent and hardy black, with robust frame and stature; but we do not find that mind and virtue, morals and feeling, depend on fairness of complexion or delicacy of form; why then, I ask, in the name of reason, should the black man have his natural liberty thrown totally down, and his body exposed to the bondage and laceration of the white? It is unjust and inhuman,—it is a foul disgrace on man,—it is an abomination in the sight of God? Of this tyranny and cruelty the prisoner has been clearly proved to be guilty, and of it the Jury ought by their verdict to convict him. This will be one great effort toward the melioration of this enslaved race, who surround us on all sides, and come almost daily into our harbour. I cannot better explain my idea of the natural rights of the African than by adopting the language of the state of Pennsylvania, when her legislature, nearly half a century ago, declared their determination to abolish slavery. They spoke thus—" It is not for us to inquire why, in the creation of mankind, the inhabitants of different parts of the world were distinguished by a difference of complexion and feature; it is sufficient to know; that we are all the work of one Almighty Hand. We find in the distribution of the human species, that the most fertile as well as the most barren parts of the earth are inhabited by men of complexion different from ours, and from each other, from whence we may reasonably, as well as religiously, infer, that he who placed them in their various situations hath extended equally his care and protection to all; and it becometh not us to counteract his mercies. We esteem it as a particular blessing granted to us, that we are enabled in this day to add one more step to universal civilization, by removing as much as possible the sorrows of those who have lived in undeserved bondage." My Lord, and Gentlemen of the Jury, reflect for a moment on the miseries of slavery, what is it that the poor African does not endure? Think of the separation of husband and wife, father and mother, children, brothers, sisters, kindred, and friends; think of the cold, the heat, the labour, and the lash, that unfeeling custom has doomed to the condition of the slave; and to whom shall he apply for redress? I glory in knowing that he can apply to British law, which, I am confident, will in this case be signally administered, by my Lord and the Jury, for the abolition of slavery. I doubt not that Heaven smiles in approbation on the efforts now making. This day will live in history, that will record this trial as the ground-work of that " universal emancipation" which it appears to be the will of the Almighty to spread, in process of time, throughout the world. Gentlemen of the Jury, you are called upon by your verdict to promote this extension of liberty to the slaves of all nations; you are prompted by your duty to God and your country to find the prisoner guilty, not out of vengeance against him, but for the sake of example, the dignity of law, the cause of nature, and the future benefit of long-injured Africa.

The Chief Justice now with perspicuity and conciseness summed up the evidence. He went through the five counts in the indictment, and shewed how they agreed with the act, and then pointed out how the evidence supported the indictment. He said the evidence appeared to him clear, conclusive, and unshaken; he would neither interest them nor delay them from discharging their duty; he was convinced they would consider the case with cool and unprejudiced minds, and a true verdict give, according to the evidence. If any difficulty occurred to them, he desired they would apply to the Court without hesitation; but legal difficulties were not within their province. The Court had already considered some, and if others were urged in proper time and place, they would be minutely investigated. It is the duty of the Judge to preserve the legal rights of the prisoner.

The Jury, after a short consultation, returned a verdict of Guilty.

On the 9th of April, CHARLES HICKSON was tried for the same offence, and acquitted by the Jury.

On the 10th, the prisoner Samo, being brought up for sentence, his counsel moved the Court on a point of law, in arrest of judgment, of which cursory notice has already been taken. Mr. H*****s, Samo's counsel, said, that, with due submission, he must again beg leave to address the Court; that in indictments the books clearly laid it down, that they should state a certain day on which the offence had been committed; now the indictment against Samo, the prisoner, takes in several months, without specifying a particular day; therefore this latitude, in point of time, must be considered as fatal to the indictment, from the opinion of the highest legal authorities. The indictment must be considered as having a flaw in it, and be quashed accordingly. These observations, the prisoner's counsel thought, could not fail to have weight on the minds of the Court in behalf of the prisoner, especially when it was remembered that Samo was apprehended at the Isle de Loss, a place out of the jurisdiction of this Court. The prisoner's counsel said he would leave the observation with the Court, and move in arrest of judgment on another ground. The prisoner was not, he said, an English subject, and therefore was not amenable to the British laws; he was a subject of Holland, and on that account was not obliged to observe the acts made in England for the abolition of the slave trade, and could not be tried legally under the 51st of George III, chap. 23., under

which he was indicted, as that act only applied to
British subjects; that the prisoner was a Dutchman
his counsel said would appear from the proofs that
would be adduced of his speaking Dutch, and of his
knowing events in Holland which passed when he was a
boy, and which he had conversed about with gentlemen
years before, who would give it in evidence. Samo also
had a Dutch passport, which was considered very sufficient proof of his nationality; his counsel, therefore,
hoped, that, under these circumstances, the Court would
not pronounce judgment on the prisoner.

Witnesses were called up, and Mr. Vaneck was sworn.
He believed Samo to be a Dutchman, because he spoke
good Dutch, and had often talked to him about Holland,
and events of the civil war in that country.

Mr. Walter Robertson swore, that he was inclined to
believe Samo was a Dutchman, on grounds similar to that
which supported the belief of Mr. Vaneck.

A passport was also produced, purporting to be from
Surinam to New York; this was attentively examined by
the Chief Justice, and returned to the prisoner's counsel.
Surinam was at the time the passport. was dated in the
possession of the Dutch.

Mr. Biggs then rose on the part of the Crown, and
said—My Lord, in reply to the arguments of the prisoner's
counsel in arrest of judgment, that, though they were forcible, they are not convincing; the *onus probandi* lies in
the prisoner; he asserts he is a Dutchman; he must prove
it; how has this proof been attempted? By shewing that
Samo can speak Dutch, knows something that passed
years ago in Holland, and has a Dutch passport. Indeed,
my Lord, speaking Dutch is no proof of being a subject
of the Prince of Orange. Knowledge of events which
happened in Holland may be known to an Italian; history,

E

hearsay, or actual sight, may furnish such information,
but whether one or all, it does not prove the prisoner to
be a Dutchman. It is asserted that the prisoner was apprehended out of the jurisdiction of this Court; that
assertion cannot be maintained, as the Isles de Loss are
considered the dependencies of Sierra Leone; they are
inhabited and cultivated by British subjects, who consider,
and have always acknowledged themselves amenable to
British laws. I can prove beside this, my Lord, that the
prisoner has often boasted of being a British subject; and
this boast is now recorded in the Sierra Leone Gazette,
and has never been contradicted by the prisoner. As to
the Dutch passport, upon which so much reliance is placed,
money could procure that for any one in a Dutch colony;
besides, this passport, admitting its validity, does not describe either the person or profession of the reputed posses-
sor, nor does it contain his christian name; it is not impossible that this passport might have been drawn up for one
of the many Samo's who reside in London, where the name
is very common among the Jews born in the neighbourhood of Duke's Place. In answer to the remarks of the
prisoner's ingenious counsel, that no day is stated in the
indictment, I beg leave to remind him that this was objected to in the early part of the trial; but if the indictment had then been quashed, a new one would have been
preferred, in which the day would appear, as I could prove
that Samo shipped off slaves on the 12th of January, 1812.
I shall conclude, my Lord, with a citation from Vatel, who,
in his work on the Laws of Nations, has a passage much in
point with the matter in discussion. The learned author,
in page 162, section 75, speaking of cases where an individual of one nation has injured the sovereign of another
nation, says, that if the offended state has in her power
the individual who has done the injury, she may not scruple
to bring him to justice, and punish him. If he has escaped,

and returned to his own country, she ought to apply to the sovereign to have justice done in the case. Now, my Lord, the prisoner at the bar has done an injury to the state; that is, he has violated the laws of England, and if even he had proved himself a Dutchman, by the law of nations we have a right to punish him, nor, as Vatel has it, shall we scruple about the matter. On this ground then, my Lord, I submit to the Court whether, as the prisoner has been found guilty of a felony, the judgment of the Court can be legally arrested? I beg that the affidavits of Mr. Alexander M'Cawley and Mr. Philip Gordon may be read, and they will be found to support the statement I have made. The affidavits were read, and it appeared that the prisoner had declared himself to be a British subject; and when it was, on some particular occasion, proposed to him to become a citizen of the United States, he publicly avowed he was an Englishman, and said he never would deny his country; and it also appeared that the prisoner had not claimed Holland as the place of his birth till he shuddered at the punishment consequent on slaving.

The CHIEF JUSTICE said the points in arrest of judgment were strong and clearly put; as to the prisoner's being a foreigner, and not within the reach of the statute, it could not be allowed. Two persons swore they believed him to be a Dutchman, and two others swore that they consider him an Englishman, and that he considered himself an Englishman till very lately. A passport from Surinam to New York is produced, but it does not state the prisoner to be a Dutchman. The prisoner has domiciled above sixteen years in the Rio Pongas; this may be considered foreign dominions, but the chiefs of that country consider the white men as British subjects, and they also consider themselves British subjects; they have claimed, in cases of distress, British protection, and received it; they purchase, reside, and trade as British subjects, not as Africans. The prisoner has derived every advantage and protection from the English law; he must not now violate it with impunity; we cannot suffer this state of oscillation; is he one moment to be within the pale of our laws and protection, and the next out of the pale of its coercion? Under the strict rule of considering indictments, I allow this one to be faulty, but precision as to dates cannot be attained where the inhabitant marked time by the number of moons, the rainy or the dry seasons, or the entrance of a man of war into the river. Even one of the best witnesses did not know the name of the month in which he celebrated Christmas. If we attended to the same exactness of day and date required in England, it is not the blessing of English jurisprudence we should bring into Africa, but the curse of legal precision; for no offender could be convicted. I conceive the indictment to be as precise as the modes, customs and manners, and information of the inhabitants, would allow; as to the prisoner's having resided in a foreign country, whose laws were the rule of his conduct, and that he is not to be brought before a tribunal whose authority he does not acknowledge, I cannot allow to be a fair statement; I have already shewn that he must be considered as a British subject, and amenable to our law; but English law is the rule of action even in the Rio Pongas. The conduct of the white inhabitants is regulated, and all their dealings in trade determined by its rule : the legislature considered this difficulty when they allowed us to try offenders against the 51st of the King, chap. 23., according to the ordinary course of law, or by the 25th of Henry the Eighth, or the 33d of the same reign, or the 11th and 12th of William the Third, British subjects have been tried in England for acts committed against the British law in Asia, in America, in Africa, and the Dutch settlement at the Cape of Good Hope, and in Europe in the center of the French government. The indictment could not be quashed.

Proclamation being made to keep silence in the Court, the learned Judge in a solemn and impressive manner addressed the prisoner in these words:—Samuel Samo, you are placed at this bar to receive the sentence of the law as a convicted felon. The philanthropy of Great Britain having determined her to abolish the barbarous and inhuman traffic in slaves, allotted pains, penalties, and confiscations, to prohibit its continuance; but finding these ineffectual, established it felony by the 51st of the King, chap. 23., either to pursue it in any shape, or to aid and assist others in carrying it on. Under the act of parliament you have been arraigned, tried by an excellent jury, and found guilty. You have had every aid the best counsel in the colony could afford you, and every benefit the law could extend to you. It now remains for the Court to pronounce the sentence which the act directs. I feel myself awfully impressed by the responsibility of my situation. This statute has left great discretionary power in the breast of the Court; the period for transportation under fourteen years, and the power of reducing the punishment to three years labour and confinement, is submitted to its direction; but in this case, there was neither evidence in your favour to induce, nor recommendation from the Jury to justify a diminution of punishment; yet your counsel have pressed forcibly on the feelings of the Court. You are the first convicted under this act, and England will anxiously look for such an example to be made, as will infuse terror and dismay into the minds of every remaining slave factor on these coasts. The penalty of the law is not death, but it is worse, for it reduces the convict to the most infamous degradation of life. Should you be sentenced to labour, you would be clothed with a peculiar cap, jacket, and trowsers, to designate your disgraceful state, and you must labour on the wharf or fort with a fetter and log appended to some limb, to prevent your escape. Yet, when we consider the crime, the punishment cannot be considered severe; for what can be more abominable than seizing, selling, and transporting human beings, without any crime against God or man being imputed to them? Our conduct in life is directed by three laws—the law of opinion, the law of the land, and the law of God. You have violated them all; the slave trader is execrated in society, and the law of opinion, would condemn you to solitude; the verdict of the Jury, under which you now wait the sentence of the Court, is declaratory of your violation of the law of the land, and your conscience must convict you of despising the law of God; think of the commandment, "Thou shalt not steal;" it is neither money nor fame, but liberty of which you have robbed your fellow-creatures. Human beings, created and made after God's image, you have stolen; you have loaded them with irons, plunged them into slavery, and bartered them for the wretched gratification of appetite and avarice; you have not, perhaps, seized on the person yourself, but you have received and sold the stolen body, and that is worse. Consider another great commandment of the Almighty, "Thou shalt do no murder." How many innocent victims have expired at your threshold; how many torn from their country, parents, or children, have you condemned to disease, to decrepitude, to slavery, and to death?—"There is a God, all nature cries aloud," that marks the movements of this world, and brings us to account; when you are summoned before that great tribunal for judgment, and those unfortunate Africans, whom you branded on the thigh with burning implements of torture, shall arise in evidence against you, what can you expect from the seat of Supreme Justice? You cannot exclaim, O God, the mercy which I have shewn to others that mercy shew to me!" Yet all that I dare do I will do in mercy. It is not an individual victim of the law that is most valuable. The annihilation of this diabolical traffic is the victim to the law that we demand. Your sentence shall be deferred until the first day of the next sessions, in the hope of finding such exertions made by your friends to extirpate this trade, as will in a great measure diminish, though they may not be able to eradicate it. And in proportion to the contrition exhibited, and the zeal for its destruction manifested, the discretion which the law gives to the Court shall be extended to you; and if it appears evidently the intention of the other slave factors, in the vicinity of this colony, to lead a new life, and turn benevolent and industrious, I will use my influence with the amiable personage at the head of this Government to extend the royal mercy to you on this laudable, salutary, and necessary repentance. Let it be done quickly and extensively—let that baneful commerce which has so long retarded the civilization, diminished the population, and dimmed the glory of Africa, be destroyed—let it be shattered to atoms in a storm of benevolent charity for mankind—it will be an immolation acceptable to the Deity—it will be a sacrifice of human viciousness on the altar of Divine compassion—it will be a death unto sin—and a new birth unto righteousness—it will plead your pardon in this life, and plead for mercy in life everlasting.

Let the prisoner be conveyed to the jail from whence he came, and there held in close confinement until the first day of the next sessions of oyer and terminer, when he shall be brought to the bar of the Court, to receive the sentence prescribed by law for the crime of which he stands convicted. Samo was immediately re-conducted to prison.

The Conclusion of the TRIAL *of* SAMO, *in a Letter from a Gentleman at Sierra Leone to an Advocate for the Abolition in London.*

Sierra Leone, July 21, 1812.

DEAR SIR,

I WILL now give you the sequel of this important trial. On the 11th of June, Samuel Samo was brought up for judgment. The merciful suggestion contained in the address of the honourable Chief Justice to the prisoner when he was remanded, was improved by the friends of Samo, who, from his long residence in the Soosoo nation, his wealth, and extensive business and connection, was an object of consequence. Though Samo had never been beloved, (and, indeed, what slave trader could be?) he was respected; and it would be no presumption in him to expect that his friends, whether Europeans or natives, would make great exertions to save him from enduring the penalty he had so justly incurred. Some time previously to the day appointed for receiving his dreadful and ignominious sentence, several petitions were humbly tendered to his Excellency Governor Maxwell, praying for the pardon of the prisoner. Three of these petitions were written in Arabic, one from the King of the Mandingo nation; one from the King at the Isles de Loss, and one from Mungo Catty, King of the Soosoo nation. The remaining two petitions were in English; one from the European settlers in the Soosoo nation, and the other from the British settlers at the Isle de Loss. A future occasion will be taken to make the whole of these interesting documents public. The Arabic petitions abound with tenderness and originality. For the present, it will suffice to remark, that they were all written in the language of pathos, sincerity, and submission, and bound the petitioners to abandon the abominable slave traffic, and to do all in their power to bring it to a total termination, upon the condition that Samo should be discharged by virtue of the royal pardon, and restored to his friends. To have the "father of the trade," converted into its avowed enemy, and all his African connexion solemnly pledged to assist him in the humane work of abolition, was a great point gained, and infinitely preferable to sacrificing an individual slave trader to the rigour of the law. Governor Maxwell, having consulted the Chief Justice, determined that he would exercise the delightful prerogative with which he was invested, of extending the royal pardon to the unhappy convict.

On the day appointed, Samuel Samo was put to the bar to hear the sentence the law directs for the crime of which he stood convicted. Mr. Biggs moved, in arrest of judgment, that the royal pardon might be read, which being done by the Clerk of the Crown, the learned Chief Justice addressed the prisoner in a manner that not only impressed him, but moved every heart in the Court. He enjoined, and explained the gratitude the prisoner ought to feel at being released from a most ignominious punishment, which, from his age and frame, must have accelerated a death, whose terrors (from the habits of his life) he must be unprepared to encounter. He mentioned, that on a former occasion he had stated many of the miseries the negro suffered, from the moment he was caught till he was shipped, to all of which the slave factor was accessary. The horrid scenes the prisoner must have witnessed on board a ship in the Rio Pongas, when the slave factors were carousing at dinner with one William Browne, (master of a Liverpool slave ship) might have deterred him from this pursuit. The rum in the cabin being exhausted, a person was dispatched to the hold to open a fresh cask

F

which caught fire from a candle; the ship was soon in flames; the inebriated factors saved themselves in their boats. Twenty-five slaves, not in irons, were drowned, and above seventy in irons, in the hold, were consumed to ashes! yet one of the wretches who was present, and who had just returned from the Matanzas, had assured him (the learned Judge) that the miseries he saw the negroes suffer in Cuba, so far exceeded any thing he imagined, that he had determined to decline the trade for ever.

He next spoke of the ship Caracai, that had been sent to Bahia with eleven hundred slaves; five hundred died on their passage, and of the six hundred landed, it was not supposed many could survive. A vessel that had foundered at sea, and the whole cargo of slaves perished, while the master and the men escaped in the boats, was also dwelt upon, and the pangs thus wantonly caused by the trade in human flesh, forcibly impressed on the recollection of the prisoner. The barbarous cruelties practised by Huggins and Hodge, in the West Indies, were very properly referred to with the indignation and abhorrence they are calculated to excite; when he described the negro woman under the torturing lash becoming a mother, every spectator seemed to be convulsed. " Conceive," said the learned Judge, " the mandate of this miscreant monster obeyed, until the offspring of unhallowed joy was prematurely precipitated from the source of life into the valley of death!" Here he made an apostrophe on the English law, and described justice in defence of the poorest African boy, dragging the richest West India planter to the bar, and from thence to the scaffold.

After depicting these scenes of horrid cruelty, his Lordship remarked, that if there were no slave factors, the unoffending, unprotected beings of Africa would not be seized, and torn from their native land, from those whom they loved, and from every thing estimable in life, to a market, to be sold! The poor slaves were first caught by the chiefs in their wars promoted by Europeans; they were then sold to the slave factors, who again bartered them for a monstrous profit, without any stipulation as to their destination or usage. No; to the avaricious slave dealer, it matters not what becomes of the wretched victim whom he sells, except that the sooner they are destroyed, the greater will be the demand for them. " Which of you slave factors," continued the learned Judge with energy, " can declare you have not transported, or caused to be transported, those very mortals whose sufferings I have described? And how many thousands are there whose miseries have not reached me, and whom you have barbarously sold into slavery? What happiness can you have in life, if you have any reflection? What recompense can you make to man for the horrors you have caused, though in the possession of the wealth of worlds? or what atonement for your peace can you make with God? None, but by repentance. Then, let it be perfect, and immediate; for, as it belongeth to him justly to punish sinners, so it is ingenerate in him to be merciful to them that repent. You have received the mercy of the royal pardon—May your future conduct deserve that of our Father who is in Heaven!

Such is the substance of the address of the Chief Justice on this memorable occasion. I pretend not to perfect description. I felt too much to attend to words. Dr. Heddle, who was on the bench, wept almost the entire time the Chief Justice spoke; and my own mind was too much engaged to observe well, or to describe accurately.

The joy expected for the pardon of Samo was turned into sadness; and on the prisoner's discharge being proclaimed, he withdrew amidst a death-like silence.

I am, dear Sir,

Your obedient humble servant.

THE TRIAL

OF

JOSEPH PETERS,

Indicted for trading in Slaves, and tried at Free-
town, before the Hon. Robert Thorpe, L.L.D.,
Chief Justice of Sierra Leone, &c.

THIS was an indictment against Joseph Peters for violating the 51st of George III. chap. 23, by selling and
bartering certain natives of Africa, who were sold for the
purpose of being treated, used, dealt with, and transferred
as slaves.

The Court met on the 11th of June, 1812; on the indictment being read by the Clerk of the Crown, the prisoner pleaded Not Guilty.

MR. BIGGS, as counsel for the Crown, opened the case
with lamenting, that notwithstanding the general promul-
gation of the laws against the slave trade, it should still be
practised, and that too under the very eye of the government, which was most active and prompt to discover the
offenders and bring them to punishment. The evidence
to be heard, would prove that the prisoner had very lately
sold several unhappy Africans into slavery; and that, in
fact, these victims of his avarice were persons over whom
he had not even the shadow of rightful authority, much
less had he a property in them, as is sometimes absurdly
and inhumanly said, when speaking of the Blacks. It
would, the counsel was sorry to state, be found, that the
prisoner at the bar had not one circumstance in his favour,

which he could plead in mitigation of the sentence due to
the aggravation of his crime. It is known that he had
been a surgeon's mate on board of one of his Majesty'
vessels ; he had been nearly six years in a medical capacity
in the employ of the proprietors of Bance Island factory,
and he was receiving British pay for attendance on British
troops, at the very time he was daily violating the slave
felony act ; thus acting with practical ingratitude towards
the country from which he derived his subsistence. The
evidence will prove that the prisoner sold or bartered from
the island of Tasso, five, if not six, African persons, who
were to be treated as slaves, and for whom he received a
valuable consideration. It will also appear that he removed, or caused to be removed, nearly forty unfortunate
Africans, who were transported from one place to another,
expressly to be treated and dealt with as slaves ; and
moreover, that the prisoner did receive the benefits of their
unrewarded labour. Should the evidence impress the
mind and conviction of the jury, as it did that of the counsel for the crown, they could not, however painful it might
be, discharge their duty, without finding a verdict of
Guilty.

MR. BIGGS went on further to observe, that there was
still a circumstance of which particular notice should be
taken. The Court would recollect what his Lordship had
said from the bench on a former occasion, at the trial of
Charles Hickson, respecting the manner of swearing some
of the witnesses. There were many of them, in the present case, similarly situated with those who gave testimony
in behalf of Hickson. Though they believed devoutly in
the existence of an infinite Providence, and entertained a
solemn sense of moral accountability ; yet they possessed
not the religion of Christ. Interpreters were in the court,
who understood all their languages, and would faithfully
interpret what the witnesses should give in testimony.

Here the Court immediately enjoined from the bench, the practice which it had efficaciously ordered before. His Lordship said, " To make the engagement or obligation conscientiously binding is the great object of an oath. Swear each witness according to the custom of his country and the religion he possesses; infuse into his mind, that by the solemnity he has gone through, he is to tell the truth, and nothing but the truth. We cannot by any other mode so securely affect the conscience of these poor people, they all believe in a Supreme Being, and acknowledge he is an avenger of falsehood, and a rewarder of truth, but they have no generally established form of worship."

The witnesses for the Crown were then brought forward.

Banta, a Timmany man, was sworn. He was sworn according to the custom of the Timmany nation; he swore by his mother, and wished she might die if he did not speak the truth, and he hoped that God might strike him dead as the earth (on which he rubbed his two forefingers and applied the dust to his tongue) if he did not relate the whole truth. *Banta* then declared that he knew the prisoner at the bar, that he knew he took slaves from the island of Tasso; he called them, ordered them away, and they were not seen afterwards at Tasso. The slaves were taken from Tasso in a canoe; he (the witness) did not know what became of the slaves, but he knows some of them were sent to Dallamoodoo, (a chief on the Boolam shore). The witness knew that Blacks, by the names of *Borogo, Yanyatta, Katta, Coosin, Yusinge* and *Yusinge's* daughter, *Screse* and his wife and a child of *Bontoe's*, were sent off by the prisoner from Tasso. The canoe in which the slaves were taken away, belonged to Bance Island. The slaves were forced off by the prisoners, whom the witness said had often beaten the slaves.

Dallamoodoo was then called up to give his evidence.

This witness was an intelligent chief reigning in the Boo-lam country, he spoke English well; he was sworn on the Koran, with great solemnity: and proceeded to state, that he knew the prisoner at the bar personally. He then produced a letter signed by the prisoner, desiring the wit-ness to catch the slaves who had run away from Tasso. The letter was dated in December, 1811. The letter was read, and the hand-writing of the prisoner proved. The prisoner also acknowledged the letter. *Dallamoodoo* de-clared further, that he had brought twenty-eight slaves to a place called Sery, a short distance above Bance Island, in the Sierra Leone river; the prisoner gave in payment for his trouble in causing the slaves to be hunted out, three women slaves, one man slave, and a child. The witness considered these persons given to him in payment, and he conceived them as his property, and that he might treat them in every way as the rest of his slaves. He said five slaves were given by the prisoner to King *Murra Brimer*, in payment for his causing the runaways from Tasso island to be caught, at the instance of the prisoner. These per-sons were given to be treated in the same manner *Murra Brimer* treats all his other slaves. The witness did not know of the prisoner's selling slaves in the Soosoo nor in the Boolam countries. Four of the black people whom he brought back were given to the witness, as payment, and one slave was given to him from Tasso. They were de-livered to him at Sery. If the witness and *Murra Brimer* had not caused the slaves to have been caught, on the re-quisition of the prisoner, the runaway blacks would not have been detained by the native chiefs of the countries into which they fled.

Tom Krooman was sworn in the same way as *Banta*, the first witness heard in this case. He knew the prisoner, and knew of his sending the black people from Tasso; they did not return back while the witness was there.

Duboo was sworn on the Old Testament; he believed in a state of future rewards and punishments. He saw many of the Tasso slaves working on William Tufft's place; they laboured as slaves, but the witness did not know of the prisoner having sent any slaves away.

Yangyarra was sworn in a very solemn manner, according to his nation, by praying that God would cause the earth to open and receive him, if he told not the whole truth. He declared he was a head man at the island of Tasso He had kept an account of the slaves sent off by the prisoner at the bar; he produced a handful of small stones, and counting out thirty, swore that was the number sent away by the prisoner. He saw the prisoner go to Sery with some slaves, who did not return. He saw him give some slaves to *Ben Muro* of *Boolam*, as payment for something; the persons delivered were to be treated as slaves; the witness did not know of the prisoner giving any more slaves.

Adam was next sworn in the same way as *Duboo*. He knew the prisoner had sent slaves from Tasso; he gave some black people to King *Murra Brimer*; they consisted of a woman, two girls, and two boys: the witness was present when these blacks were delivered; the prisoner gave them up to be treated as slaves; he sent some to *Ben Muro;* he saw them; they were given as slaves; a man, his wife, and one girl; the witness did not see the prisoner receive any thing in return; the time was about five months ago; the prisoner, he heard, gave the slaves as payment for catching the runaways; they were given at Bance Island, and witness was present at the time.

KENNETH MACAULEY, *Esq., sworn.*

He saw three women, a man, and a child, who had been given to *Dallamoodoo* by the prisoner; he also saw at *Murra Brimer*'s five slaves, who had been delivered by the prisoner as payment for his trouble in causing the runaway negroes to be caught. *Murra Brimer* told the witness, that if the Governor of Sierra Leone would give him a thousand bars, (equal to *S*.1000), he would render up the slaves; but not without, as *Murra Brimer* declared they were his slaves.

Bondoo was sworn on the Old Testament. The prisoner gave him as a slave to *Santera*; he made his escape; he was sold by the prisoner as a slave; he was delivered by the prisoner at Bance island to *Santera*, who took him to Port Logo, together with his wife and two children, who were delivered at the same time by the prisoner at the bar. They were sent off in a canoe about four months ago; they were sold by the prisoner as slaves, who made the black people work as slaves, and flogged them; he had beaten the witness; he saw many at Port Logo who were sold by the prisoner, many of whom the witness named; they were sold as slaves.

Monday was sworn on the New Testament and on the earth. She saw the prisoner give four slaves to *Murra Brimer*, and four to *Dallamoodoo*, at the town of Sery, for catching the runaways. A *Boolam* man also got four slaves: he lives at Sery; they were all to be treated as slaves; it was four months since they were delivered; the witness did not know whether slaves were disposed of before they ran away from Tasso. The prisoner sent a woman slave, named Çainbosco, to the *Soosoo* country, and received a bill in pay for her. She has heard the prisoner say he had sold slaves for rice; he said he would sell whom he pleased of the Tasso people; he threatened to sell her, and had beaten her.

Quiepa knelt down and kissed the earth, and was thus sworn to tell the truth. He knew the prisoner had sent slaves from Tasso; he saw him sell one slave for three goats, three sheep, one bull, and a ton of salt; the prisoner sold a yellow girl to *Dallamoodoo*; *Duboo* brought the girl away, and afterwards went with her to the *Soosoo* country, she was sent by the prisoner from Tasso; the prisoner sold *Banko*, a black woman; she was sold for rice, but only four belies (about two bushels) were received; the woman was sent to *Murury*, in the river Rochelle. The prisoner gave four slaves to King *Murra Brimer*, as payment for catching the Tasso runaways.

Saree was sworn by his mother, and the earth. The prisoner, this witness declared, had sent five slaves to *Dalla-moodoo*; he saw them; *Brimer* got four slaves; he knew a woman sold by the prisoner, and sent to Angofa; *Duboo* took her; the prisoner saw the witness sell a man to *Benmura*, saw him sold at Bance island, nearly seven months ago; the prisoner delivered the man, and Benmura took him away; he saw bullocks, sheep, and goats, given to the prisoner for slaves, who were all delivered over to be treated as slaves, and continue in slavery.

[Here Duboo was called again by the Court.]

He said he carried a woman, by order of the prisoner, to Tombee, in the Soosoo country; he received for her half a ton of salt, one bull, three goats, and three sheep; he delivered these articles to William Tufft, who is the prisoner's partner; William Tufft delivered the girl, or woman, to him; the prisoner was present, who is considered an higher man than Tufft. It was three months since the witness went with the woman sold, he took her from Bance island; he received also from the prisoner another woman to sell, and he received three at another time to take to William Tufft. The prisoner sent two boys to Boolam; they were to be given to Tufft's sister as slaves; five other slaves were sent to Tufft, a boy, a man, his wife, and two children.

Boreega sworn according to the custom of his nation. The prisoner at the bar, he said, had sold him to Dalla-moodoo; he did not know what was given for him; he was sent to the *Soosoo* country as a slave; the prisoner sent him from Tasso to Bance island, where he put him into chains, ordered him into a boat, and sent him off; he was sent to Melega; he was not one of the runaways who were brought back; the irons cut his wrists and ancles till the blood ran from them; he worked hard as a slave for the prisoner at the bar, and was flogged by him.

Foosingbag sworn in the custom of her nation. The prisoner, she declared, had sold her to Dallamoodoo; she was treated as a slave; she saw Borago (whom the prisoner also sold) in irons, in the canoe going off. The prisoner had the command over them, and the witness heard him say he would sell whom he pleased; he sold her mother and two children to Murra Brimer; they were sold by the prisoner's direction.

Katta sworn. She was sold with her mother at Bance island; the prisoner ordered her from Tasso, and sold her; she ran away, was brought back, and given to Dallamoodoo.

Samuel Scott sworn. The people sent by the prisoner to Boolam were, a boy, two women, and a child; the prisoner gave three men to Benmura; they were delivered at Bance island. The prisoner gave to Murra Sery, two women, a child, and a boy, as a recompense for his trouble; they were given to be dealt with and treated as slaves; the witness considered that the prisoner assumed the chief authority at Bance island and at Tasso.

Boree was sworn by God, his mother, and the earth. The prisoner desired him to build a town for William Tufft; he gave the witness a wife, then took her away, and sold her. He complained of losing his wife, and the prisoner said he would sell him as he had done his wife, and that he would send him after her; the prisoner told the witness he had sold his wife to a *Mandingo* man; his wife was taken from him at one of the houses he had built for William Tufft; she is with Murra Brimer; it is three months since she was sold; he saw the prisoner give many slaves away, but does not know what he received for them. Some were sent to Benmurra, some to Murra Brimer, and some to others; they were sent to be dealt with as slaves; the prisoner and William Tufft acted together as one person.

The evidence on the part of the Crown here closed — The prisoner had no witnesses to call. When called on for his defence, he said the blacks were his enemies, and all they had said was false; that he had nothing to do with Bance island nor Tasso, and that he was not accountable for what might have been done with the slaves by the acting agent of that place. He said he was innocent, and hoped the Court would believe him.

Mr. Biggs addressed the Court and Jury with but a few words in closing the case; he said that it was clearly obvious, that the indictment was confirmed by the testimony in all its bearings, and that the Jury could not, when they duly reflected on the acts of illegality, and the scenes of oppression and cruelty which had just been laid open, hesitate about giving a verdict against the prisoner.

The learned Chief Justice recapitulated the laborious mass of evidence, and after several brief and appropriate remarks, left the Jury to the proper effect of clear and sound testimony upon their duty and consciences.

The Jury very soon returned a verdict of GUILTY.

There was nothing pleaded in arrest of judgment; and the prisoner was sentenced to *Seven Years Transportation*.

The Trial of WILLIAM TUFFT came on the day following that of Peters. The same witnesses were again brought forward, and sworn. Among the whole there was no disagreement or incongruity of testimony. Tufft's indictment was the same in substance with that of Peters', and it clearly appeared that he had throughout been an accessary with Peters, and had in some instances acted from his own authority. His object was proved to have been, to appropriate the labour of the Bance island and Tasso blacks to his own use and profit, and to dispose of their persons whenever it suited his own convenience or anger, or that of his associate Peters. This William Tufft is a black man, who had been educated in England, and had lived as a servant in the family of a nobleman near Windsor. When he was put on his defence, he only pleaded that he acted by the orders of Peters, and of the acting agent of Bance island; but even this unavailing plea was not supported by evidence. He was sentenced by the learned Chief Justice to *Three Years hard Labour* on the public works at Sierra Leone.

Thomas Wheeler, acting agent at Bance island, was tried under an indictment, the following day, as being deeply implicated in the illegal practices of Peters and Tufft; but the whole of the witnesses in the preceding trials declared, that, as far as they knew, the prisoner was innocent; and Dallamoodoo, the principal witness, went away the night before the trial, and could not be got back to give his testimony; he said he was fearful of offending the Kings of the surrounding countries, by appearing again in a court against slave traders, Mr. Wheeler was consequently acquitted.

During the examination of the witnesses in this case, the firm of Messrs. John and Alexander Andersons, of London, was several times mentioned. Mr. Wheeler produced a letter, signed by these gentlemen, which, on being read, reflected great honour on them, while it aggravated the guilt of the convicts Peters and Tufft; as it appeared

that the proprietors of Bance island had written to Mr.
Wheeler, their acting agent, expressing their desire that
their black people should be no longer treated as slaves, and
should be allowed to live at liberty on any of the islands
around Bance island, and to subsist by their industry on
lands, and to live in the houses belonging to their late
masters. It was given in evidence that this letter had been
read to Peters and Tufft, but they had kept it secret from
the negroes, which clearly manifested their intention of
treating them and disposing of them as slaves.

———

Sierra Leone, August 18, 1812.

DEAR SIR,

If my former letter excited expectation, I
hope it may not be disappointed by this. You have now
before you the novel trials recently concluded in this colony; many important reflections will very naturally be
suggested to you on this subject; but as I am on the spot,
and have had my mind attentively occupied on the present
condition of this part of Africa, you will not consider the
remarks which I am about to make either obtrusive or out
of time.

It seems to me, that no person in England of common
curiosity, or habits of thinking, can pass over these trials
without pleasing and serious sensations. We are here
presented with a scene interesting in an unusual degree.
In the case of the pardoned slave trader, we see the apprehension of a man, who had for upwards of sixteen years
been in the constant practice of bartering and transporting his fellow-creatures for rum, tobacco, and gunpowder. This is an object that cannot be indifferent to
the coldest heart. Figure to yourself this man brought to
the tribunal of justice, and there pleading innocence.
Observe the progress of the evidence, and hear how slave

trading is systematized in Africa, notwithstanding the most powerful nation on earth is pledged to abolish slavery.

That this trial is most important must be confessed, because we have the foundation now laid on which may be erected the superstructure of African emancipation; and a precedent is confirmed to discover and punish those who would continue to obstruct it. In the excellent address of the learned Chief Justice to the prisoner, he remarks, " that it is not the individual victim of the law that is the most valuable," but that " the annihilation of the diabolical traffic is the victim the law demands." I was extremely gratified when I heard this sentiment advanced; because it justified me in believing that the Chief Justice did not wish to sacrifice Samo merely as the first slave trader convicted, but desired, on the contrary, if possible, that he should be pardoned, upon conditions that would at once meet the intentions of the British Government, and benefit the interests of humanity. It is certain that judgment might have been instantly pronounced on Samo, and he might now be carrying stone at the public works, with a log to his ancle, and a driver with a whip at his back; yet, I must repeat how much better was it to have had him reserved for the interposition of his whole African connexion, who have bound themselves to renounce the commerce in slaves for ever; and, if they resume it, have exposed themselves to inevitable discovery, by a correspondence which is now established between Sierra Leone and the Soosoo nation.

It is a matter of gratification that this measure was adopted, instead of immediately condemning the prisoner to the penalties of the law. Much good will flow from this exercise of clemency; and I am persuaded that the Chief Justice, in the act of reservation, both served the cause and honour of his country, and gratified the naturally humane disposition of his own heart. It is really

surprizing and gratifying to contemplate the great body
of work that has been done in this colony for effecting the
abolition in a period comparatively so small. If we survey
the whole of the operations which have been gradually
going forward to help Africa, since the year 1788, we shall
discover that the exertions of a few months in 1812 sur-
pass them all. The restrictions put by law on the slave
trade, from time to time, certainly deserve great commendation, because they were grounded on goodness and
humanity, and their benefits were practically known to
the poor enslaved African; but may we not be permitted
to inquire, without presumption, why humanity has moved
in a slow and heavy step when it might have sped with
rapid flight, bearing all the blessings benevolence could
bestow. The cause, in my estimation, is no other than the
same general one, which produces nearly all the mischief and
misery in the world—the love of money, with its concomi-
tant power. Can there be any other reason shewn why the
same measures which are now in force for the extirpation
of the slave trade should not have been adopted thirty
years ago? The trade was then equally cruel and barbarous, equally disgraceful to man, and detestable in the
sight of Heaven, as it is now rightly considered; but the
merchant, the planter, and the factor, have been enriched
by this lucrative commerce in their fellow-creatures, and
they have received that patronage and countenance, which
wealth, however obtained or employed, is seldom denied.
The opulence accumulated by this vile trade has been pro-
digious, and a great portion of it has been monopolized
by the British slave merchants, who, from their various
facilities, were always able to procure, at the best rate, the
articles adapted to the African market. These articles
were, and still are, bartered for human beings. This subject shall be for future enlargement. The trials will show
to what expedients the slave trader has resorted, and how
thoroughly they have been exposed and defeated by the

regular interposition of the law. But there are still other discoveries to be made, and other punishments to be inflicted, before this business can be made complete. There is ground to believe, that in England there are persons who have promoted the slave trade by their connexion in the neighbourhood of this colony, while they professed to abhor it. When these characters shall have been brought to light, we shall have many strange and wicked facts to contemplate; and Africa will know its real enemies in the exposure of certain of its hypocritical friends. But all that England can do to break up the trade in human flesh will be of no avail, if her allies be allowed to carry it on. Portugal, it is true, is confined by treaty to trade for slaves only within her own dominions on the coast; but this is not the case with Spain. The subjects of this nation still send their vessels for cargoes of slaves; and they affect astonishment at being told, that they are not at liberty to ship them off from every part of Africa. In the island of Teneriffe, both British and American vessels are put under Spanish colours, and then they imagine they may trade in slaves with impunity. At St. Jago, the Portuguese flag is supplied to English and American vessels for the same purpose. Among the variety of places which I visited on the coast of Africa was that of the Portuguese settlement of Bissao. From this place was once shipped a great number of slaves; and though its commerce is now much reduced, it still obstructs the benevolence of the British Government, in putting down the slave commerce. The inhabitants at Bissao have been habituated from infancy to slaving, and from the local situation of the country it is evident, that so long as it continues in the same hands, the trade on the windward coast cannot be totally abolished. This subject I shall resume at a future occasion.

To omit the praise due to the navy on this coast would

be improper and unfair. The Hon. F. P. Irby, in the Amelia frigate, commands on this station. He is very truly entitled to great commendation for his vigilance and zeal in capturing slave traders, and his success has been considerable. Captain E. Scobell, in the Thais; Lieutenant G. Mitchene, in the Protector; and Lieutenant W. R. Pascoe, in the Daring, have all manifested an extremely laudable activity to detect and capture vessels which have resorted to this coast for slaves; and I should hope their enterprize and success would certainly obtain them promotion.

In the great aim of an entire destruction of the slave trade on this coast, I am happy to say, there is a perfect union of sentiment between the three principal persons in this colony. The Governor, the Chief Justice, and the Commodore, have their minds stimulated into action by the same motive, and firmly concentrated and directed to the accomplishment of the same object. I hope this object will at last be consummated; for, when I consider the qualities, the power, and the honours, which distinguish England from and above all other nations, I am filled with astonishment that she does not interest herself more effectually in behalf of the suffering African. I am not satisfied that the best means are made use of to abolish the detestable traffic in slaves. With regard to England, on this subject, her national religion, her constitution and policy, are directly repugnant to every species of cruelty or oppression, and consonant with just and national liberty; why then, I would ask, should she be lukewarm in extending the range of these invaluable blessings? This, I believe to be the time to follow up with more effectual plans those which have already been acted upon, for conferring an increased portion of happiness on this country. It is granted that England is desirous to remove the curse that has so long pressed on Africa; it will then appear a

circumstance of great satisfaction to every humane heart,
that, for the attainment of this object, a more fit character
could not have been selected than the present Chief Justice
of this colony, than whom no man can be a more determined
hater of slavery. In the cause of African emancipation,
he has exhibited the deepest zeal, patiently and indefati-
gably devoted; notwithstanding the multiplicity of business to which he has to attend as Chief Justice, he has an
ear ever ready to hear the complaint of the suffering
African, and his humanity affords him prompt redress.
Though he is exposed to all the injuries incident to residing
in a deleterious climate, this has no terror for him while
he is busied in dispensing the blessings of British law in
favour of a people who have too long been the victims of
the lawless. He is certainly entitled to the thanks of his
country.

You will recollect that, previous to my leaving England,
we had often spoken of Africa, and lamented the unhappy
state of that country. In these conversations we were
always cordial. This concurrence of sentiment not only
sanctions and invites, but urges me to call your attention
to the observations which I may be enabled to make during
my visit to Africa. Though I do not mean to continue
very long in this dreadful climate, I shall be industrious
to obtain all the knowledge I possibly can, relative to the
colony and those connected with it. It is, I assure you, a
very different place from what it has been represented by
certain persons in England. A great error prevails with
regard to the nature of the climate, which has been styled
good even in the face of parliament; but I do, from experience and attentive observation, pronounce it to be one
of the worst, if not exclusively the worst, climate on
earth; and no European can reside in it many months,
without having his constitution essentially impaired.

I would advise the immediate publication of the report of the trials, which I send now, because they will do good, by spreading useful information. The letters which grew out of this occasion, I submit to your discretion. If you think they contain matter of sufficient interest to be made public, I lay no injunction on you to withhold them; and in this view you may consider these communications as the precursor and introduction of a series of letters respecting this country and colony, which, I think, the novel state of Africa will shortly justify, being collected under the title of *The African Register.*

I am, dear SIR,

Your very obedient servant,

Printed by James Gillet, Crown-court, Fleet street, London.

THE

FUGITIVE SLAVE CIRCULARS.

A SHORT ACCOUNT

OF THE CASE OF SOMMERSETT THE NEGRO, AND OF
LORD MANSFIELD'S CELEBRATED JUDGMENT, UNDER WHICH
SLAVERY IN ENGLAND RECEIVED ITS DEATH-BLOW.

ALSO OF

FORBES *v.* COCHRANE,

EXTENDING THE DOCTRINE OF SOMMERSETT *v.* STEUART
TO SLAVES ON BOARD BRITISH PUBLIC SHIPS, WITH A
NOTE OF OTHER CASES ON THE SUBJECT.

Full reprints of Sommersett *v.* Steuart, and Forbes *v.* Cochrane.
Copies of the original and amended Fugitive Slave Circulars, with a
reference to the Slave Trade Acts of 1873, and a note as to the
right of searching slave vessels.

BY

HENRY GEORGE TUKE, ESQ.,

OF THE INNER TEMPLE;

BARRISTER AT LAW.

LONDON:

STANFORD, CHARING CROSS.

1876.

CHELTENHAM :

PRINTED BY HORACE EDWARDS,

396, HIGH STREET.

PREFACE.

In the Session of Parliament now commencing, much debate will certainly take place on the subject of the "Fugitive Slave Circular," issued, revoked, and re-issued in the course of the last few months.

Those who have constantly at hand for ready reference the weighty volumes on international and constitutional law, or the State Trials, and other reports containing "Sommersett's Case," and "Forbes v. Cochrane," the leading cases on the subject of slavery and fugitive slaves, are, beyond professional circles, comparatively few.

The present pamphlet, containing a full reprint of those cases, is therefore issued, as it is hoped, conveniently supplying a want. It professes, however, to be no more than a compilation to meet a special occasion. A short summary of each of the leading cases is prefixed for the use of those whose time is unusually limited, as also a brief account of other cases bearing on the subject; an explanation of some terms not of every-day occurrence; a reprint of the "Fugitive Slave Circulars;" and, in reference to the slave trade generally, a short notice of the Slave Trade (Consolidation) and the Slave Trade (East African Coast) Acts, 1873. To these is added a note on our present right of searching slave vessels.

With the exception of the famous case, "Forbes v. Cochrane," we do not find in our books any other, in which the claim for damages for taking away slaves who have come on board public ships, or ships of war, either on the high seas, or (*a*) within the territorial waters of another state, has ever been tried out, but, we do find, that the almost universal opinion of the publicists, and writers on international law, is in favour of the extra-territoriality of such ships, within the waters of other states, and we thus assume with confidence that it exists, as to such ships, and those on board, to a very great extent. (*b*)

Whether to the almost infinite extent, just now so vehemently claimed for it, and so as to make free, slaves who get on board of such ships, and, claim their freedom on the argument, that, being there is tantamount to being on British land, will at least have to be calmly discussed. We cannot settle it on generous impulse only.

Even with regard to slaveholding states themselves, detestable as is the institution of slavery, when we remember that we profess to put down the foreign export of slaves, and, not as yet to interfere with " domestic slavery," there may be some element of justice in the outcry of (perhaps hereditary) owners of domestic slaves, at a sudden loss of their services,

---

(*a.*) The note to Forbes *v.* Cochrane treats the case as one where fugitive slaves from a plantation in Florida had got on board a British ship of war on the *high* seas—vide Reprint. It appears that this ship of war was anchored about a mile from Cumberland Island, off the coast of Georgia. On a careful scrutiny of the best maps the author has been able to inspect, this situation, if the southern end of Georgia is intended, has all the appearance of being within three geographical miles of the part of Florida then belonging to Spain, and so within the territorial waters of the latter. If so, however, this makes the decision in Forbes *v.* Cochrane the stronger and the more confirmatory of the general and popular view, in the present discussion. Mr. Justice Best, however, in effect, states that his opinion would have been different had the ship been in Spanish waters.—ED.

(*b.*) " The state of international law on the subject of *private* vessels in foreign ports, is judiciously explained by Mr. Halleck, in his treatise, pp. 171-2. It may be said to be this : So far as regards acts done at sea before her arrival in port, and acts done on board in port, by members of the crew to one another, and so far as regards the general regulation of the rights and duties of those belonging on board, the vessel is exempt from local jurisdiction ; but, if the acts done on board affect the peace of the country in whose port she lies, or the persons or property of its subjects, to that extent that State has jurisdiction. The local authorities have a right to visit all such vessels, to ascertain the nature of any alleged occurrence on board. Of course, no exemption is ever claimed for injuries done by the vessel to property or persons in port, or for acts of her company not done on board the vessel, or for their personal contracts, or civil obligations, or duties relating to persons not of the ship's company."
Vide Wheaton, 8th Ed., by Dana, p. 154, s. 96, Note.

without any compensation whatsoever. A midnight flitting of such domestic slaves, on to the deck of a British man-of-war, and their so becoming free, not only within their late owners territorial waters, but it may be within a harbour, and, at but a few yards distance of the house they fled from, must be certainly calculated to arouse bitter feelings, and yet, can scarcely be called a forced illustration of what may happen, if the law contended for by so many public speakers, is as they put it.

If we admit, that, petty seaboard states of Africa and other countries, are nations within the meaning of international law (c), now that, owing to many recent treaties, we have really no great power to dispute with on this question of slavery, we must be especially careful to avoid any steps which may "painfully have the look of mere vis major," and trust to more legitimate means for securing the end we have in view.

That many small seaboard states of Africa are treated as entitled to a voice on questions of slavery, is clear from the Slave Trade (East African Coasts), Act 1873, and the Slave Trade (Consolidated), Act, 1873 ; both of which in defining a foreign state with which we may have a treaty, say—" the term 'foreign state' includes any foreign nation, people, tribe, sovereign, prince, *chief or headman.*"

(c.) Mr. Wheaton, (8th Ed. by Dana, p. 117, sec. 11,) says : " Is there a uniform law of nations ? There certainly is not the same one for all the nations and states of the world. The public law, with slight exceptions, has always been, and still is, limited to the civilized and Christian people of European origin ; but, quoting Montesquieu (p. 18, sec. 12,) he continues : Montesquieu, in his *Esprit des Lois,* says that 'every nation has a law of nations—even the Iroquois, who eat their prisoners, have one. They send and receive ambassadors ; they know the laws of war and peace ; the evil is, that their law of nations is not founded upon true principles.' At p. 22, sec. 13, Mr. Wheaton remarks, that 'the more recent intercourse between the Christian nations in Europe and America, and the Mohammedan and Pagan nations of Asia and Africa, indicates a disposition on the part of the latter to renounce their peculiar international usages, and adopt those of Christendom. The right of legation has been recognized by, and reciprocally extended to Turkey, Persia, Egypt, and the States of Barbary.' And since then, says Mr. Dana, in a note (p. 22), ' The most remarkable proof of the advance of Western civilization in the East, is the adoption of this work of Mr. Wheaton, by the Chinese Government, as a text-book for its officials, in International Law, and its translation into that language in 1864, under imperial auspices.' "

IV

In the writer's belief there are many persons who look upon slavery as *piracy*, and are impatient at the idea of international law prevailing in the case of slave owners and their vessels, but as a fact, although in the case of subjects of Great Britain, and by Acts of Parliament, or by treaties, slave dealing is made piracy in many cases, with severe penalties, it has not yet been declared to be so, and is not so by the law of nations.

In the case of "The Louis," Lord Stowell, in 1817, referring to the slave trade, says, "To make it piracy or a crime, by the universal law of nations, it must have been so considered and treated in practice by all civilized states, or made so by virtue of a general convention."

"The slave trade, or the contrary, had been carried on by all nations, including Great Britain, until a very recent period, and was still carried on by Spain and Portugal, and not yet entirely prohibited by France. It was not, therefore, a criminal act by the consuetudinary law of nations; and every nation, independently of special compact, retained a legal right to carry it on. No nation could exercise the right of visitation and search upon the common and unappropriated parts of the ocean, except upon the *belligerent* claim. No one nation had a right to force its way to the liberation of Africa by trampling on the independence of other states; or to procure an eminent good by means that are unlawful; or to press forward to a great principle by breaking through other great principles that stand in the way."

The extent of our rights of search for slave vessels being also frequently over-rated, a copy of Mr. Dana's note, summing up the latest conclusions on the subject, will, it is hoped, be found useful, and will be seen at the end of this pamphlet.

Reverting, however, to the question of the circulars that were recently issued, the second of these seeming at length fully to admit the freedom of slaves who find their way on board British ships on the *high* seas, and being only faulty in this respect, as to the detailed directions given to our naval officers, there will remain but the question of the freedom of such slaves coming on board our public ships, without collusion or enticement, within territorial waters, and in *any* place within such waters.

The facts which have led to so much excitement, will presently be before us. That, the discussion, under more grave responsibility, which is about to ensue, will lead to some better understanding on the subject, to treaties and agreements with the chieftains of the seaboard states, resulting in a more extensive abatement, or abolition of slavery, must be the earnest wish of us all.

To our gallant naval officers, it is at least due, that the responsibilities they often incur, should be, as far as possible, clearly defined. That these are, not only in such cases as are now being discussed, but in the course of their work in suppressing the slave trade generally, very considerable, will appear from the clauses in the Acts of 1873, which will be presently set out.

Cheltenham,
   5th February, 1876.   H. G. TUKE.

ERRATA.

Page 2, line 38.—For " villien "—read " villein "

Page 3, line 21.—For " whatsoever ; and he then submitted, not "—
read "whatsover ;" and he then submitted, "not "

Page 6, line 9.—For " judgement," read "judgment "

Page 8, line 17.—For " ports " of the sea—read " parts " of the sea

Page 13, line 33.—-For "Slavery local law," read "Slavery is a local law"

SOMMERSETT'S CASE,

AND OF THE

SPEECH OF MR. HARGRAVE, HIS COUNSEL.

A.D. 1771.

SOMMERSETT, an African Negro, had been taken to Virginia as a slave, and there sold to Mr. Charles Steuart, a resident gentleman. At that date slavery was lawful in Virginia, and accordingly Steuart became the legal owner of Sommersett. He brought Sommersett to England to serve him during a temporary residence here, intending to carry him back to America when his business was completed. But, whilst in London, Sommersett absented himself, and refused to return with Steuart to America. Thereupon Steuart had him seized and delivered to John Knowles, commander of the Ann and Mary, lying in the Thames, with instructions to convey him to Jamaica, and sell him as a slave. Knowles confined Sommersett in irons, and was about to take him to Jamaica, when a habeas corpus was granted by Lord Mansfield, C.J., directed to Knowles, requiring him to return the body of Sommersett, and show cause for detaining him.

Lord Mansfield having referred the matter to the decision of Court of Queen's Bench, Sommersett was brought before the Court in Hilary Term, 1772. Whereupon, Knowles having set out the facts on affidavit, openly avowing them as stated, Mr. Hargrave, counsel for Sommersett, in a most masterly speech, dealt with the case under two different aspects.

1st.—As to Mr. Steuart's right to the person of the Negro.

2nd.—As to his authority, assuming he had such right, to enforce it, by forcibly detaining Sommersett and transporting him out of the kingdom as proposed. On the first point "whatever," said Mr. Hargrave, " Mr. Steuart's right may be, it springs out of the condition of slavery in which the negro was before his arrival in England, and wholly depends on the *continuance* of that relation ; the power of imprisoning at pleasure here, and of transporting into a foreign country for sale as a slave, certainly not being exerciseable over an ordinary servant. Accordingly the return fairly admits slavery to be the sole foundation of Mr. Steuart's claim."

Mr. Hargrave then suggests another way in which the return might have been speciously framed as if Sommersett had been a mere servant, and he then, after dealing with the various definitions of slavery, and an exhaustive and most interesting review of its origin, nature, and incidents, and of its gradual decline in Europe, between the eighth and fourteenth centuries, alludes to its introduction into America from Africa, through the Portuguese, in 1508 ; and of the unsuccessful efforts of the Emperor Charles V. to stay its progress.

After an explanation of the origin, varieties, and expiration of villenage in England, he thus proceeds. "From the 15th of James I., being more than 150 years ago, the claim of villenage has not been heard of in our Courts of Justice, and nothing can be more notorious than that the race of persons who were once the objects of it, was about that time completely worn out by the continual and united operation of deaths and manumissions."

Then after a still further exposition of the former methods of making title to a villien, with an argument that the state of the law excluded a new slavery, and that such could not be permitted in face of the extinction of villenage, nor even under the laws of

England against slavery by contract, he examines
the cases, quotes dicta of the Judges, states and
answers objections, and, coming to the question of
attempting to obtrude this new slavery into England,
he thus proceeds :—" And here it will be material to
observe that if on the declension of slavery in this
and other countries of Europe where it is discountenanced, no means had been devised to obstruct the
admission of a new slavery, it would have been vain
and fruitless to have attempted superseding the ancient
species. But I hope to prove that our ancestors at
least were not so short-sighted ; and that long and
uninterrupted use has established rules as effectual to
prevent the revival of slavery, as their humanity was
successful in once repressing it. I shall endeavour to
show that the law of England never recognized any
species of domestic slavery, except the ancient one of
villenage, now expired, and has sufficiently provided
against the introduction of a new slavery under the
name of villenage, or any other denomination whatsoever", and he then submitted, "not merely that negroes
become free on being imported into this country, but that
the law of England confers the gift of liberty, entire and
unincumbered, not in name only, but really and
substantially ; and consequently that Mr. Steuart cannot have the least right over Sommersett the negro,
either in the open character of a slave, or in the
disguised one of an ordinary servant."

Incidentally, in this first part of his argument,
Mr. Hargrave touches the question of "lex loci," and
the argument that slavery of negroes being then
lawful in America, even under English acts of Parliament, the lex loci ought to prevail, and that the
master's property in the negro as a slave having had a
lawful commencement in America, could not be justly
varied by bringing him into England. Whether the
Lex loci shall prevail against the law of England, as
presently found to be established in Sommersett's case,
and claimed to exist on board H. M. ships of war, or
public ships, being the subject about the details of

which so hot a contention is now raging; and, as for
" Great Britain," we shall presently read " British ship
of war" or "public ship," it may be as well to set
out Mr. Hargrave's argument under this head in full.
" I shall," says he, " answer the objection by explaining
the limitation under which the lex loci ought always
to be received."

"It is a general rule that the lex loci shall not
prevail if great inconvenience will ensue from giving
effect to it. Now I apprehend that no instances can
be mentioned in which an application of the lex loci
would be more inconvenient than in the case of
slavery. It must be agreed that where the lex loci
cannot have effect without introducing the thing
prohibited in a degree either as great or nearly as
great as if there was no prohibition, then the greatest
inconvenience would ensue from regarding the lex loci,
and consequently it ought not to prevail. Indeed by
receiving it under such circumstances the end of a
prohibition would be frustrated either entirely or in a
very great degree; and so the prohibition of things
the most pernicious in their tendency would become
vain and fruitless. And what greater inconvenience
can we imagine than those which would necessarily
result from such an unlimited sacrifice of the municipal
law to the law of a foreign country? I will now
apply this general doctrine to the particular case of
our own law concerning slavery. Our law prohibits
the commencement of domestic slavery in England,
because it disapproves of slavery, and considers its
operation as dangerous and destructive to the whole
community. But would not this prohibition be wholly
ineffectual if slavery could be introduced from a
foreign country? In the course of time, though
perhaps in a progress less rapid, would not domestic
slavery become as general, and be as completely
revived in England by introduction from our colonies
and from foreign countries, as if it was permitted to
revive by commencement here; and would not the
same inconveniences follow? To prevent the revival

of domestic slavery effectually, its introduction must be resisted universally, without regard to the place of its commencement; and therefore, in the instances of slavery, the lex loci must yield to the municipal law. From the fact of there never yet having been any slavery in this country, except the old and now expired one of villenage, it is evident that hitherto our law has uniformly controlled the lex loci in this respect; but so long as the same policy of excluding slavery is retained by the law of England, it must continue entitled to the same preference. Nor let it be thought a peculiar want of complaisance in the law of England, that disregarding the lex loci in the case of slaves, it gives immediate and entire liberty to them when they are brought here from another country."

" Most of the other European states, in which slavery is discontinued, have adopted a like policy."

Mr. Hargrave then proceeds to his second point, viz., assuming Mr. Steuart's right in this country to Sommersett as a slave, had he authority to enforce that right by transporting him out of England, and he forcibly argued that there being in this country no other laws but the laws of villenage, Mr. Steuart could take advantage of no other, and they restrained the Lord from forcing the villein out of England. "The law," he said, "under which the Lord's power over his villein was thus limited, had reached the times in which he was speaking. It is a law made William I., and the words of it are ' prohibemus ut nullus vendat hominem extra patriam.' "

Mr. Hargrave's argument was thus eloquently concluded :—

" By condemning the return, the revival of domestic slavery will be rendered as impracticable by introduction from our Colonies and from other Countries as it is by commencement here. Such a judgment will be no less to the public advantage than it will be conformable to natural justice, and to principles and authorities of law ; and this court, by effectually obstructing the admission of the new slavery of negroes into England will in these times reflect as much honor on themselves as the great judges, their predecessors, formerly acquired by contributing so uniformly and successfully to the suppression of the slavery of villenage."

NOTE.—For the speeches of other counsel engaged pro and con., the reader is referred to the full report of the case.

Lord Mansfield, on June 22nd, 1772, delivered his judgement, which will be found in full in the reprint of the case presently set out ; but a quotation of its conclusion may prove useful in this place. " The only question before us," said Lord Mansfield, " is whether the cause on the return is sufficient. If it is, the negro must be remanded ; if it is not, he must be discharged. The return states that the slave departed and refused to serve ; whereupon he was kept to be sold abroad. So high an act of dominion must be recognized by the law of the country where it is used. The power of the master over his slave has been extremely different in different countries. The state of slavery is of such a nature that it is incapable of being introduced on any reasons, moral or political, but only by positive law, which preserves its force long after the reasons, occasions, and time itself from whence it was created, are erased from the memory. It is so odious that nothing can be suffered to support it but positive law. Whatever inconveniences therefore may follow the decision, I cannot say this case is allowed or approved by the law of England ; and therefore the black must be discharged."

This judgment was the death blow of actual slavery in this country, and we now purpose to give a short explanation of the terms " lex loci," " territorial waters," and some other matters, and then to consider how far the decision in this great case affected slaves found in our colonies, and incidentally on board our British ships-of-war, or public ships.

THE "LEX LOCI" AND "MUNICIPAL LAW."

The law known as the "Lex Loci" being so frequently alluded to in "Sommersett *v.* Steuart," it may be well here to point out for the information of the general reader, that this is the law of any particular place or state, as to which a nation such as England stands in the position of a foreign nation, whilst by "municipal law," when an Englishman speaks of it, is intended the law of this latter.

Thus an Englishman talking of the law of his own country which he is under at home, or in visiting, let us say, on board a British ship, the port of some African independent state, talks of it as the Municipal Law—that of his own state—his own law,—whilst he speaks of the local law of the African independent state and of its territorial waters, when he comes within them—and of which presently—as the Lex Loci, or law of that particular state or place.

A British vessel in a port of such a state, and within its territorial waters, in some respects maintains the municipal law of its own country on board, in some respects comes under the "lex loci."

"The municipal institutions of a state," says Wheaton, 8th Ed., by Dana, p. 153, "may also operate beyond the limits of its territorial jurisdiction," when he instances the case of ambassadors, and proceeds— "If there be no express prohibition, the ports of a friendly state are considered as open to the public armed and commissioned ships belonging to another nation with whom that state is at peace. Such ships are exempt from the jurisdiction of the local tribunals and authorities, whether they enter the ports under the license implied from the absence of any prohibition, or under an express permission stipulated by treaty. But the private vessels of one state, entering the ports of another, are not exempt from the local jurisdiction, unless by special compact, and to the extent provided by such compact."

Thus we see, that our municipal law may have a temporary residence, or effect, in the very harbours and territorial waters (presently defined) of another state, with the " lex loci " prevailing all around it.

On the high seas, and beyond the territorial limits of any other state, the public and private vessels of every nation are subject only to the jurisdiction or municipal law of the state to which they belong.

TERRITORIAL WATERS.

These words, so familiar to writers on international law, and to members of our naval and mercantile marine services, may perhaps here deserve a few words of explanation.

" By the generally approved usage of nations," says Wheaton, " which forms the basis of international law, the maritime territory of every state extends.

1stly—To the ports, harbours, bays, mouths of rivers, and adjacent parts of the sea, inclosed by headlands belonging to the same state.

2ndly—To the distance of a marine league,* or as far as a cannon shot will reach from the shore along all the coasts of the state.

3rdly—To the straits and sounds bounded on both sides by the territory of the same state, so narrow as to be commanded by cannon shot from both shores, and communicating from one sea to another."

These definitions will be sufficient for our present purpose. On the coast of England in certain localities, called " Kings Chambers," in the Baltic, on the Coast of Denmark, in the Bosphorus, Black Sea, and Dardanelles, and in other parts of the world, there are exceptional provisions sanctioned by long usage—the law of nations—or treaties as to particular waters ; but with these we are not immediately concerned, and may consider the definitions of Wheaton quoted above

---

* Three Geographical Miles.

as generally applying to all countries forming parts of Africa, America, or elsewhere, where and with which questions as to slavery are likely to arise.

High . seas may of course be generally defined as the seas distant more than a marine league, or cannon shot from the shore, although with the change in the power of modern projectiles, the latter part of the definition may perhaps some day have to be reconsidered.

FORBES v. COCKRANE.

AT the trial of this case, before Abbott, C.J., at the London sittings after Trinity Term, 1822, a verdict was found for the plaintiff, damages £3,800, subject to the opinion of the Court above, on the case, of which the following is an outline :—

The Plaintiff, Forbes, was a British merchant in Florida, part of the dominions of the King of Spain, who was in amity with Great Britain. Forbes was proprietor of a cotton plantation near the River St. John, and of above 100 slaves employed upon it. During the then late war between Great Britain and America in February, 1815, Vice Admiral Sir A. Cockrane, one of the defendants, was Commander-in-Chief of H. M. ships on the North American Station. The other defendant, Rear Admiral Sir G. Cockburn, was second in command, and his flag ship the " Albion." The British forces had taken possession of Cumberland Island, and at that time occupied and garrisoned the same. The Albion, Terror Bomb, and other ships of war formed a squadron, under Sir G. Cockburn's immediate command off Cumberland Island where the headquarters of the expedition were. Sir A. Cockrane was at a considerable distance to the southward of Cumberland Island. In 1814, a proclamation had been published by the said Sir A. Cockrane, as such Commander-in-Chief, and Sir G. Cockburn, had received great numbers of copies thereof, whilst the ships under his command were lying off the Chesapeake, and distributed them at the Chesapeake amongst the different ships, but none were distributed by the order of the defendant, Sir G. Cockburn, to the southward of the Chesapeake, the

southern extremity of which is full 400 miles distant
from Cumberland Island. The proclamation stated
that it had been represented to him, Sir A. Cockrane,
"That many persons then resident in the United
States had expressed a desire to withdraw therefrom,
with a view of entering into his Majesty's service, or
of being received as free settlers into some of his
Majesty's colonies; and it then notified that all those
who might be disposed to emigrate from the United
States, would, with their families, be received on board
his Majesty's ships of war, or at the military posts
that might be established upon the coasts of the
United States, where they would have their choice
of either entering into his Majesty's sea or land forces,
or of being sent as free settlers to the British
possessions in North America, or the West Indies,
where they would meet with all due encouragement.
One of these proclamations was seen on Amelia
Island, East Florida, which is less than a mile from
Cumberland Island, and about 30 miles from Forbes'
plantation. In the night of the 23rd Feb., 1815, a
number of Forbes' slaves deserted from his plantation,
and on the following day thirty-eight of them were
found on board the Terror Bomb, part of the squadron at Cumberland Island, and entered on the
muster-books as refugees from Saint John's. On the
26th of the same month of February, Sir G. Cockburn
received from the plaintiff a memorial, stating that the
plaintiff had been a resident in the Spanish provinces
of East and West Florida for nearly thirty years, as
clerk and partner of a mercantile house established
under the particular sanction of the Spanish government, for the purpose of trade with the southern
nations of Indians, and which they were allowed to
continue by special permission from his Brittanic
Majesty, pending the two Spanish wars that occurred
during that period. The said mercantile house had
acquired considerable property in these provinces, and
particularly the cotton plantation and slaves. That on
the night of the 23rd instant, sixty-two of his said

negroes deserted from his plantation, of whom he had found thirty-four, on board his Majesty's ship Terror. But that the said slaves refused to return to their duty, under pretence that they were then free, in consequence of having come to this island in possession of his Britannic Majesty. The plaintiff therefore prayed that Sir G. Cockburn would order the said thirty-eight slaves to be delivered to him, their lawful proprietor. A correspondence took place. Forbes, who had leave to do so from Sir G. Cockburn, endeavoured to persuade the slaves to go back, without avail. Sir A. Cockrane subsequently, after further correspondence, directed Sir G. Cockburn to send them to Bermuda, where he took them, in the Albion. The slaves who were taken on board the Albion were worth to Forbes £3,800. Comyn, counsel for the plaintiff, and Jervis for defendants, having ably argued the case—

Bayley, J., Holroyd, J., and Best, J., in turn delivered judgment, and unanimously in favour of the defendants. In the course of his judgment, Mr. Justice Holroyd spoke thus : " The law of slavery is, however, a law in invitum, and when a party gets out of the territory where it prevails, and out of the power of his master, and gets under the protection of another power, without any wrongful act done by the party giving that protection, the right of the master, which is founded on the municipal law of the particular place only, does not continue, and there is no right of action against a party who merely receives the slave in that country, without doing any wrongful act. This has been decided to be the law with respect to a person who has been a slave in any of our West India colonies, and comes to this country. The moment he puts his foot on the shores of this country his slavery is at an end. Put the case of an uninhabited island, discovered and colonized by the subjects of this country ; the inhabitants would be protected and governed by the law of this country. In the case of a conquered country, indeed, the old laws would prevail, until altered by the king in council ; but in the case of the newly discovered country, freedom would be as much the inheritance of the inhabitants and their children as if they were treading on the soil of England. Now, suppose a person who had been a slave in one of our own West India settlements escaped to such a country, he would thereby become as much a freeman as if he had come into England. He ceases to be a slave in England only because there is no law which sanctions his detention in slavery ; for the same reason he would cease to be a slave the moment he landed on the supposed newly discovered island. In this case, indeed, the fugitives did not escape to any island belonging to England, but they went on board an English ship (which for this purpose may be considered a floating island), and in that ship they became subject to the English laws alone. They then stood in the same situation in this respect as if they had come to an island colonized by the English. It was not a wrongful act in the defendants to receive them, quite the contrary. The moment they got on board the English ship, there was an end of any right which the plaintiff had by the Spanish laws acquired over them as slaves. They had got beyond the control of their master, and beyond the territory where the law recognizing them as slaves prevailed ; they were under the protection of another power."

And Mr. Justice Best, in his much admired and oft quoted judgment, after remarking that "these slaves were not seduced from the service of their employer by any act of the defendant's—if they had been, the case would have been very different,"—proclaimed, "Slavery local law, and therefore, if a man wishes to preserve his slaves, let him attach them to him by affection, or make fast the bars of their prison, or rivet well their chains, for the instant they get beyond the limits where slavery is recognised by the local law, they have broken their chains, they have escaped from their prison, and are free. These men when on board an English ship, held all the rights belonging to Englishmen, and were subject to all their liabilities. If they had committed any offence, they must have been tried according to English laws. If any injury had been done to them, they would have had a remedy by applying to the laws of this country for redress. I think that Sir G. Cockburn did all that he lawfully could do to assist the plaintiff; he permitted him to endeavour to persuade the slaves to return, but he refused to apply force. I think that he might have gone further, and have said that force should not be used by others; for if any force had been used by the master or any persons in his assistance, can it be doubted that the slaves might have brought an action of trespass against the persons using that force? Nay, if the slave, acting upon his newly recovered right of freedom, had determined to vindicate that right, originally the gift of nature, and had resisted the force, and his death had ensued in the course of such resistance, can there be any doubt that every one who had contributed to that death would, according to our laws, be guilty of murder? That is substantially decided by Sommersett's case, from which it is clear that such would have been the consequence had those slaves been in England; and so far as this question is concerned, there is no difference between an English ship and the soil of England; for are not those on board an English ship as much protected and governed by the English laws as if they stood upon English land? If there be no difference in this respect, Sommersett's case has decided the present; he was held to be entitled to his discharge, and consequently, all persons attempting to force him back into slavery would have been trespassers, and if death had ensued in using that force, would have been guilty of murder. It has been said that Sir G. Cockburn might have sent them back. He certainly was not bound to receive them into his own ship in the first instance, but having done so, he could no more have forced them back into slavery than he could have committed them to the deep."

And after an exhaustive treatment of the case, the learned judge thus concludes : " The place where the transaction took place was, with respect to this question, the same as the soil of England. Had the defendants detained these men on board their ships near the coast of England, a writ of habeas corpus would have set them at liberty. How then can an action be maintained against those gallant officers for doing that of their own accord which, by process of law in a British court of justice, they might have been compelled to do ? I have before adverted to the narrower ground upon which this case might have been decided, but if slavery be recognized by any law prevailing in East Florida, the operation of that law is local. It is an anti-Christian law, and one which violates the rights of nature, and therefore ought not to be recognized here. For these reasons I am of opinion that our judgment must be for the defendants."

Judgment for the defendants.

As bearing on the decision in Sommersett's case the following cases have been decided :—

THE SLAVE GRACE.

2 Hagg. Adm. R. 94.

In 1822, Mrs. Allan, of Antigua, came to England, bringing with her a female slave, Grace, who, whilst in England did not claim her freedom, but returned to Antigua with Mrs. Allan, and there continued to act as her domestic slave ; and on a question arising as to her importation into Antigua, contrary to 59 Geo. 3, c. 120, (held, however, by Lord Stowell not to apply to England and its colonies,) and, as to whether the said Grace, being a free subject of his Majesty, was unlawfully imported as a slave from Great Britain into Antigua, and there illegally held and detained in slavery, contrary to the form of the statute in such case, made and provided. Lord Stowell determined that she had not acquired the *status* of a free person, and become so entitled to be considered in the colony. To use Lord Stowell's expression her liberty was placed " between parentheses."

DRED SCOTT.—SCOTT v. SANDFOR

19 Howard U.S,R., 393.

In this case, a slave in a state where slavery was legal, was taken by his master into another state of the Union in which slavery was prohibited by law. Nothing was done there to change his condition as a slave, and on his returning to the state he had come from, he was declared to have again become a slave.

The following case, relating to slaves in an American merchant ship being freed by coming into British waters, and getting to land, was, under special circumstances, referred to arbitration :—

THE CREOLE.

Wheaton, 8th Edition by Dana, Sec. 103, note.

The brig Creole, an American merchant vessel, sailed from a port in Virginia in 1841, bound to New Orleans, having on board one hundred and thirty-five slaves. A portion of the slaves rose against the officers, and got complete possession of the vessel, killing one passenger, and severely wounding the captain and others of the crew in the struggle.

They compelled the mate, under threat of death, to navigate the vessel to Nassau, where she arrived and came to anchor. At the request of the United States consul at Nassau, nineteen of the slaves, who were identified as having taken part in the acts of violence, were arrested by the local authorities, and held to await the decision of the British Government. As to the rest of the slaves, there was a question whether they got on shore and gained their liberty by their own act, or through the positive and officious interference of the colonial authorities, while the vessel was under control of the consul and master. ˙ Mr. Webster addressed a letter to Lord Ashburton on this subject. His position is, that " if vessels of the United States, pursuing lawful voyages from port to port along their own shore, are driven by stress of weather, or carried by unlawful force into British ports, the government of the United States cannot consent that the local authorities in those ports shall take advantage of such misfortune, and enter them, for the purpose of interfering with the condition of persons or things on board, as established by their own laws. If slaves, the property of citizens of the United States, escape into British territories, it is not expected that they will be restored. In that case the territorial jurisdiction of England will have become exclusive over them and must decide their condition. But slaves on board of

American vessels lying in English waters are not
within the exclusive jurisdiction of England, or under
the exclusive operation of English law; and this founds
the broad distinction between the cases.   If persons
guilty of crime in the United States seek an asylum in
the British dominions, they will not be demanded until
provision for such cases be made by treaty ; because
the giving up of criminal fugitives from justice, is
agreed and understood to be a matter in which every
nation regulates its conduct according to its own
discretion.   It is no breach of comity to refuse such
surrender.   On the other hand, vessels of the United
States, driven by necessity into British ports, and
staying there no longer than the necessity exists,
violating no law, and having no intent to violate any
law, will claim, and there will be claimed for them,
protection and security, freedom from molestation,
and from all interference with the character or condition of persons or things on board.

In the opinion of the Government of the United
States, such vessels, so driven and so detained by
necessity in a friendly port, ought to be regarded as
still pursuing their original voyage, and turned out of
their direct course by disaster or by wrongful violence ;
that they ought to receive all assistance necessary to
enable them to resume their direct course; and that
interference and molestation by the local authorities,
when the whole voyage is lawful both in act and
intent, is ground for just and grave complaint."—
Webster's Works, VI: 303-308.

Mr. Wheaton wrote an article upon this subject
in the Revue Française et Etrangere, ix. 345, in which
he took the ground that the Creole never passed under
British jurisdiction so as to affect the legal relations of
persons and things on board, or to give the British
Government such jurisdiction over the persons on
board as to make the case one of extradition ; and
that the master, with such aid as he could obtain from
the Consul or otherwise, was entitled not only to carry
to the United States all the persons on board, whether

held as slaves or criminals, without molestation from the authorities, but to receive the assistance of those authorities to regain and hold possession of his vessel.

The United States Government demanded the restoration of the slaves, which was refused by the British Government, on the ground that, being in fact at liberty within the British dominion, they could not be seized there when charged with no crime against British law, and while there was no treaty of extradition.

This case was then submitted, as a private claim for pecuniary indemnity, to the commission under the convention of Feb. 8, 1853. The commissioners being unable to agree, it was, by the terms of the convention, referred to an umpire, Mr. Joshua Bates of London. In deciding the case, Mr. Bates stated two propositions of law,—

First, That, as the slaves were perfectly quiet, and on board an American ship under the command of the captain, the authorities should have seen that the captain was protected in his rights over them.

Second, That "the municipal law of England cannot authorize a magistrate to violate the law of nations, by invading with an armed force the vessel of a friendly nation, that has committed no offence, and forcibly dissolving the relations which, by the laws of his country, the master is bound to preserve and enforce on board."

There would seem to be no doubt of the latter proposition, but the facts which Mr. Bates considered to be proved were hardly sufficient for its application. At the same time, they made a stronger case than was necessary for the first proposition. Although there was no "invading with an armed force, and forcibly dissolving the relation," the authorities still not only gave no aid to the master, but officially announced to the negroes that they were free to go or stay on board, and this while there were private boats alongside ready to take them off, in which were men apparently ready to resist the use of force by the master to retake them.

As to the former proposition of Mr. Bates, I do not find a course of precedents acted upon or acquiesced in by nations, and it seems open to speculation. It may be conceded, as a general statement, that local authorities ought to give active aid to a master in defending and enforcing, against the inmates of his vessel, the rights with which his own nation has intrusted him, if these rights are of a character generally recognized among all nations, and not prohibited by the law of the place. But it may well admit of doubt, whether the local authorities must give active aid to the master against persons on board his vessel who are doing no more than peacefully and quietly dissolving, or refusing to recognize, a relation which exists only by force of the law of the nation to which the vessel belongs, if the law is peculiar to that nation, and one which the law of the other country regards as against common right and public morals. The local authorities might not interfere to dissolve such relations, where the peace of the port or the public morals are not put in peril; but they might, it would seem, decline to lend force to compel their continuance. The most tenable ground for Mr. Bates' decision is, that the facts, as he found them, showed an active and officious, though not forcible, intervention by the authorities to encourage the negroes in leaving the vessel, and to discourage the master from using such means as he had to prevent it."

The following, on the immunity of public ships within the territorial waters of other states, are the leading cases in support of Forbes v. Cochrane.

REG v. LESLEY BELL. CC. 220

Mr. Broom, in his learned work on Constitutional Law, in quoting this case says, "it was judicially observed that although an English ship in some respects carries with her the laws of her country in the territorial waters of a foreign state, yet, in other respects, she is subject to the laws of that state, as to acts done to the subjects thereof. But it is clear that an English ship on the high seas, out of any foreign territory, is subject to the laws of England ; and persons, whether foreign or English, on board such ship, are as much amenable to English law as they would be on English soil."

CASE OF THE EXCHANGE.

Quoted in Wheaton, by Dana, 8th Edition, pp. 116, 154, 162, 168, 550.

From Cranch Rep., Vol. 7, pp. 135—147.

On the distinction between public and private vessels, Mr. Wheaton says (p. 161), " But certainly in practice nations had not yet asserted their jurisdiction over the public armed ships of a foreign sovereign entering a port open for their reception," and immediately referring to "The Exchange", Mr. Dana, p. 550 note, says, " In this case, an opinion of the highest order of merit was delivered by C. J Marshall. The court came to the conclusion that the vessel in question being a public armed ship in the service of a foreign sovereign with whom the United States were at peace, and having entered an American port open for her reception on the terms on which ships of war are generally permitted to enter the ports of a friendly power, must be considered as having come into the American territory under an implied promise that, while necessarily within it, and demeaning herself in a friendly manner, she should be exempt from the jurisdiction of the country."

Again, p, 168, note by Mr. Dana : " It may be considered as established law, now, that the public vessels of a foreign state coming within the jurisdiction of a friendly state, are exempt from all forms of process in private suits. Nor will such ships be seized, or in any way interfered with in judicial proceedings, in the name and with the authority of the State to punish violations of public laws. In such cases the offended state will appeal directly to the sovereign. Any proceeding against a foreign public ship would be regarded as an unfriendly, if not hostile act, in the present state of the law of nations."

SOMMERSETT'S CASE.

The Case of James Sommersett, a Negro, on a Habeas Corpus.

King's Bench : 12 George III., A.D. 1771-2.

20 STATE TRIALS.—I.

* ON the 3rd of December, 1771, affidavits were made by Thomas Walklin, Elizabeth Cade, and John Marlow, that James Sommersett, a negro, was confined in irons on board a ship, called the "Ann and Mary," John Knowles, commander, lying in the Thames, and bound for Jamaica; and Lord Mansfield, C.J., on an application, supported by these affidavits, allowed a writ of *habeas corpus*, directed to Mr. Knowles, and requiring him to return the body of Sommersett before his lordship, with the cause of detainer.

Mr. Knowles on the 9th of December, produced the body of Sommersett before Lord Mansfield, and returned for cause of detainer, that Sommersett was the negro-slave of Charles Steuart, Esq., who had delivered Sommersett into Mr. Knowles's custody. in order to carry him to Jamaica, and there sell him as a slave, Affidavits were also made by Mr. Steuart and two other gentlemen, to prove that Steuart had purchased Sommersett as a slave in Virginia, and had afterwards brought him into England, where he left his master's service; and that his refusing to return, was the cause of his being carried on board Mr. Knowles's ship.

Lord Mansfield, choosing to refer the matter to the determination of the Court of King's Bench, Sommersett, with sureties, was bound in a recognizance for his appearance there, on the second day of the next Hilary Term; and his lordship allowed till that day for settling the form of the return to the *habeas corpus*. Accordingly,

---

* This case is reported as Somerset *v.* Stewart, 1 Loffts. Mr. Howell, compiler of the Reports of State Trials, says as a preface to his report, " Of this case only a statement of facts and Mr. Hargrave's learned argument were inserted in the former edition of this work. I have here added the other arguments, andthe Judgment of the Court, from Loffts' Reports, in which is a note of the case under the name Somerset *v.* Stewart,"

on that day, Sommersett appeared in the Court of King's Bench, and then the following return was read:—

I, John Knowles, commander of the vessel, called the "Ann and Mary," in the writ hereunto annexed, do most humbly certify and return to our present most serene sovereign the king; that at the time hereinafter mentioned, of bringing the said James Sommersett from Africa; and long before, there were, and from thence hitherto there have been, and still are, great numbers of negro-slaves in Africa; and that, during all the time aforesaid, there hath been and still is, a trade, carried on by his Majesty's subjects, from Africa to his Majesty's colonies or plantations of Virginia and Jamaica in America, and other colonies and plantations belonging to his Majesty in America, for the necessary supplying of the aforesaid colonies and plantations with negro-slaves; and that negro-slaves, brought in the course of the said trade from Africa to Virginia and Jamaica aforesaid, and the said other colonies and plantations in America, by the laws of Virginia and Jamaica aforesaid and the said other colonies and plantations in America, during all the time aforesaid, have been, and are saleable and sold as goods and chattels; and upon the sale thereof, have become, and been, and are, the slaves and property of the purchasers thereof, and have been, and are saleable and sold by the proprietors thereof, as goods and chattels. And I do further certify and return to our said lord the king, that James Sommersett, in the said writ, hereunto annexed named, is a negro, and a native of Africa; and that the said James Sommersett, long before the coming of the said writ to me, to wit, on the 10th day of March, in the year of our Lord   , was a negro-slave in Africa aforesaid, and afterwards, to wit, on the same day and year last aforesaid, being such negro-slave, was brought in the course of the said trade as a negro-slave from Africa aforesaid to Virginia aforesaid, to be there sold; and afterwards, to wit, on the 1st day of August, in the year last aforesaid, the said James Sommersett, being and continuing such negro slave, was sold in Virginia aforesaid to one Charles Steuart, Esq., who then was an inhabitant of Virginia afore-said; and that the said James Sommersett thereupon then and there became, and was the negro slave and property of the said Charles Steuart, and hath not at any time since been manumitted, enfranchised, set free, or discharged; and that the same James Sommersett, so being the negro slave and property of him the said Charles Steuart, and the said Charles Steuart having occasion to transact certain affairs and business of him the said Charles Steuart in this kingdom, he the said Charles Steuart, before the coming of the said writ to me, to wit, on the first day of October, in the year of our Lord, 1796, departed from America aforesaid, on a voyage for this kingdom, for the purpose of transacting his aforesaid affairs and business, and with an intention to return to America, as soon as the said affairs and business of him the said Charles Steuart in this kingdom should be transacted; and afterwards, to wit, on the 10th day of November, in the same year, arrived in this kingdom, to wit, in London, that is to say, in the parish of St. Mary-le-bow in the ward of Cheap; and that the said Charles Steuart brought the said James Sommersett, his negro slave and property, along with him in the said voyage, from America aforesaid to this kingdom, as the negro slave and property of him the said Charles Steuart, to attend and serve him, during his stay and abiding in this kingdom, on the occasion aforesaid, and with an intent to carry the said James Sommersett back again into America, with him the said Charles Steuart, when the said affairs and business of the said Charles Steuart should be transacted; which said affairs and business of the said Charles Steuart are not yet transacted, and the intention of the said Charles Steuart to return to America as aforesaid hitherto hath continued and still continues. And I do further certify to our said lord the king, that the said James Sommersett did accordingly attend and serve the said Charles Steuart in this kingdom, from the time of his said arrival, until the said James Sommersett's departing and absenting himself from the service of the said Charles Steuart, hereinafter mentioned, to wit, at London, &c., aforesaid, in the parish and ward aforesaid; and that before the coming of this writ to me, to wit, on the first day of October, in the year of our Lord, 1771, at London, &c., aforesaid, to wit, in the parish and ward aforesaid, the said James Sommersett, without the consent and against the will of the said Charles Steuart, and without any lawful authority whatsoever, departed and absented himself from the service of the said Charles Steuart, and absolutely refused to return into the service of the said Charles Steuart, and serve the said Charles Steuart, during his stay and abiding in this kingdom, on the occasion aforesaid: whereupon the said Charles Steuart afterwards and before the coming of this writ to me, to wit, on the 26th day of November, in the year of our Lord, 1771, on board the said vessel called the "Ann and Mary," then and still lying in the river Thames, to wit, at London, aforesaid, in the parish and ward aforesaid, and then and still bound upon a voyage for Jamaica aforesaid, did deliver the said James Sommersett unto me, who then was, and yet am master and commander of the said vessel, to be by me safely and securely kept and carried and conveyed, in the said vessel, in the said voyage to Jamaica aforesaid, to be there sold as the slave and property of the said Charles Steuart; and that I did thereupon then and there, to wit, at London aforesaid, in the parish and ward aforesaid, receive and take, and have ever since kept and detained the said James Sommersett in my care and custody, to be carried by me in the said voyage to Jamaica aforesaid, for the purpose aforesaid. And this is the cause of my taking and detaining the said James Sommersett, whose body I have now ready as by the said writ I am commanded.

After the reading of the return, Mr. Serjeant Davy, one of the council for Sommersett, the negro, desired time to prepare his argument against the return; and on account of the importance of the case, the court postponed hearing the objections against the returned, till the 7th of February, and the recognizance for the negro's appearance was continued accordingly. On that day Mr. Serjeant Davy and Mr. Serjeant Glynn argued against the return, and the further argument was postponed till Easter term, when Mr. Mansfield, Mr. Alleyne, and Mr. Hargrave were also heard on the same side. Afterwards Mr. Wallace and Mr. Dunning argued in support of the return, and Mr. Serjeant Davy was heard in reply to them. The determination of the court was suspended till the following Trinity Term; and then the court was unanimously of opinion against the return, and ordered that Sommersett should be discharged.

*ARGUMENT OF MR. HARGRAVE FOR THE NEGRO.—Though the learning and abilities of the gentlemen, with whom I am joined on this occasion, have greatly anticipated the argument prepared by me; yet I trust, that the importance of the case, will excuse me for disclosing my idea of it, according to the plan and order, which I originally found it convenient to adopt.

Short state. of the case.

The case before the court, when expressed in few words, is this: Mr. Steuart purchases a negro slave in Virginia, where by the law of

---

* At the foot of the text in this account of the trial, appears this note: "The following argument on behalf of the negro is not to be considered as a speech actually delivered; for though the author of it, who was one of the counsel for the negro, did deliver one part of his argument in court, without the assistance of notes, yet his argument as here published is entirely a written composition. This circumstance is mentioned lest the author should be thought to claim a merit to which he has not the least title.—HARGRAVE."

The report in Loffts', of Mr. Hargrave's speech is very brief, and in words, though not in substance, different from that furnished by Mr. Hargrave in writing to the Editor of the State Trials, and Mr. Loffts admits that his report was not taken by himself, but at second hand, from a friend.—ED.

the place negroes are slaves, and saleable as other property. He comes into England, and brings the negro with him. Here the negro leaves Mr. Steuart'a service without his consent; and afterwards persons employed by him seize the negro, and forcibly carry him on board a ship bound to Jamaica, for the avowed purpose of transporting him to that island, and there selling him as a slave. On an application by the negro's friends, a writ of *habeas corpus* is granted; and in obedience to the writ he is produced before this court, and here sues for the restitution of his liberty.

The questions, arising on this case, do not merely concern the Importance unfortunate person, who is the subject of it, and such as are or may of the case. be under like unhappy circumstances. They are highly interesting to the whole community, and cannot be decided, without having the most general and important consequences; without extensive influence on private happiness and public security. The right claimed by Mr. Steuart to the detention of the negro is founded on the condition of slavery, in which he was before his master brought him into England; and if that right is here recognised, domestic slavery, with its horrid train of evils, may be lawfully imported into this country, at the discretion of every individual, foreign and native. It will come not only from our own colonies, and those of other European nations; but from Poland, Russia, Spain and Turkey, from the coast of Barbary, from the western and eastern coasts of Africa, from every part of the world, where it still continues to torment and dishonour the human species. It will be transmitted to us in all its various forms, in all the gradations of inventive cruelty; and by an universal reception of slavery, this country, so famous for public liberty, will become the chief seat of private tyranny.

In speaking on this case, I shall arrange my observations Points which under two heads. First, I shall consider the right which Mr. arise in the Steuart claims in the person of the negro. Secondly, I shall case. examine Mr. Steuart's authority to enforce that right, if he has any, by imprisonment of the negro and transporting him out of the kingdom. The court's opinion in favour of the negro, on either of these points, will entitle him to a discharge from the custody of Mr. Steuart.

I. The first point, concerning Mr. Steuart's right in the person 1st point— of the negro, is the great one, and that which, depending on a variety The right claimed in of considerations, requires the peculiar attention of the court. the slave's Whatever Mr. Steuart's right may be, it springs out of the condition person. of slavery, in which the negro was before his arrival in England, and wholly depends on the continuance of that relation; the power of

imprisoning at pleasure here, and of transporting into a foreign
country for sale as a slave, certainly not being exerciseable over an
Slavery, the ordinary servant. Accordingly the return fairly admits slavery to
foundation
of the claim. be the sole foundation of Mr. Steuart's claim; and this brings the
question, as to the present lawfulness of slavery in England, directly
before the court. It would have been more artful to have asserted
Mr. Steuart's claims in terms less explicit, and to have stated the
slavery of the negro before his coming into England, merely as a
ground for claiming him here, in the relation of a servant bound to
follow wherever his master should require his service. The case
represented in this disguised way, though in substance the same,
would have been less alarming in its first appearance, and might
have afforded a better chance of evading the true question between
the parties. But this artifice, however convenient Mr. Steuart's
counsel may find it in argument, has not been adopted in the return;
the case being there stated as it really is, without any suppression of
facts to conceal the great extent of Mr. Steuart's claim, or any
colouring of language to hide the odious features of slavery in the
feigned relation of an ordinary servant.

Difficulty of   Before I enter upon the inquiry into the present lawfulness of
defining
slavery.   slavery in England, I think it neeessary to make some general observations on slavery. I mean, however, always to keep in view slavery
not as it is in the relation of the lowest species of servant to his
master, in any state, whether free or otherwise in its form of government. Great confusion has ensued from discoursing on slavery
without due attention to the difference between the despotism of a
severeign over a whole people and that of one subject over another.
The former is foreign to the present case; and therefore when I am
describing slavery, or observing upon it, I desire to be understood
as confining myself to the latter; though from the connection
between the two subjects, some of my observations may perhaps be
applicable to both.

General   Slavery has been attended in different countries with circum-
observations
on domestic stances so various, as to render it difficult to give a general description
slavery.   of it.* The Roman lawyer calls slavery a constitution of the law
of nations, by which one is made subject to another contrary to
nature. But this, as has been often observed by the commentators,
is mistaking the law, by which slavery is constituted, for slavery
itself, the cause for the effect; though it must be confessed, that the

---

* The notes to this case in the State Trials are very numerous,
and some of great length, and in a publication of this nature are of
course therefore omitted.—ED.

latter part of the definition obscurely hints at the nature of slavery. Grotius describes slavery to be an obligation to serve another for life, in consideration of being supplied with the bare necessaries of life. Dr. Rutherforth rejects this definition, as implying a right to direct only the labours of the slave, and not his other actions. He therefore, after defining despotism to be an alienable right to direct all the actions of another, from thence concludes, that perfect slavery is an obligation to be so directed. This last definition may serve to convey a general idea of slavery; but like that by Grotius, and many other definitions which I have seen, if understood strictly, will scarce suit any species of slavery, to which it is applied. Besides, it omits one of slavery's severest and most usual incidents ; the quality, by which it involves all the issue in the misfortune of the parent. In truth, as I have already hinted, the variety of form. in which slavery appears makes it almost impossible to convey a just notion of it in the way of definition. There are, however, certain properties which have accompanied slavery in most places; and by attending to these, we may always distinguish it from the mild species of domestic service so common and well-known in our own country I shall shortly enumerate the most remarkable of those properties, particularly such as characterise the species of slavery adopted in our American colonies, being that now under the consideration of this court. This I do, in order that a just conception may be formed of the propriety with which I shall impute to slavery the most per nicious effects. Without such a previous explanation, the most solid objections to the permission of slavery will have the appearance of unmeaning, though specious, declamation.

Slavery always imports an obligation of perpetual service; an obligation, which only the consent of the master can dissolve. It generally gives to the master an arbitrary power of administering every sort of correction, however inhuman, not immediately affecting the life or limb of the slave ; sometimes even these are left exposed to the arbitrary will of the master; or they are protected by fines, and other slight punishments, too inconsiderable to restrain the master's inhumanity.—It creates an incapacity of acquiring, except for the master's benefit.—It allows the master to alienate the person of the slave in the same manner as other property.—Lastly, it descends from parent to child, with all its severe appendages.—On the most accurate comparison, there will be found nothing exagger ated in this representation of slavery. The description agrees with almost every kind of slavery, formerly or now existing , except only that remnant of the ancient slavery, which still lingers in some parts

Properties usually incident to slavery.

of Europe, but qualified and moderated in favour of the slave by the humane provision of modern times.

Bad effects of slavery.

From this view of the condition of slavery, it will be easy to derive its destructive consequences.—It corrupts the morals of the master, by freeing him from those restraints with respect to his slave, so necessary for control of the human passions, so beneficial in promoting the practice and confirming the habit of virtue.—It is dangerous to the master; because his oppression excites implacable resentment and hatred in the slave, and the extreme misery of his condition continually prompts him to risk the gratification of them, and his situation daily furnishes the opportunity.—To the slave it communicates all the afflictions of life, without leaving for him scarce any of its pleasures; and it depresses the excellence of his nature, by denying the ordinary means and motives of improvement. —It is dangerous to the state, by its corruption of those citizens on whom its prosperity depends; and by admitting within it a multitude of persons, who being excluded from the common benefits of the constitution are interested in scheming its destruction.— Hence it is, that slavery, in whatever light we view it, may be deemed a most pernicious institution : immediately so to the unhappy person who suffers under it; finally so to the master who triumphs in it, and to the state which allows it.

Opinions of some modern writers in favour of slavery under many restrictions.

However, I must confess, that notwithstanding the force of the reasons against the allowance of domestic slavery, there are civilians of great credit, who insist upon its utility; founding themselves chiefly on the supposed increase of robbers and beggars, in consequence of its disuse. This opinion is favoured by Pufendorf and Ulricus Huberus. In the dissertation on slavery, prefixed to Potgieserus on the German law *De statu servorum*, the opinion is examined minutely and defended. To this opinion, I oppose those ill-consequences, which I have already represented as almost necessarily flowing from the permission of domestic slavery; the numerous testimonies against it, which are to be found in ancient and modern history; and the example of those European nations, which have suppressed the use of it, after the experience of many centuries and in the more improved state of society. In justice also to the writer, just mentioned, I must add, that, though they contend for the advantages of domestic slavery, they do not seem to approve of it in the form and extent in which it has generally been received, but under limitations, which would certainly render it far more tolerable. Huberus, in his Eunomia Romana, has a remarkable passage, in which, after recommending a mild slavery, he cautiously distinguishes

it from that cruel species, the subject of commerce between Africa
and America. His words are:—*Loquor de servitute, qualis apud
civiliores poputos in usu fuit; nec enim exempla barbarorum, vel quæ
nunc ab Africa in Americam fiunt hominum commercia, velim mihi
quisqaam objiciat.*

The great origin of slavery is captivity in war, though sometimes
it has commenced by contract. It has been a question much agitated
whether either of these foundations of slavery is consistent with
natural justice. It would be engaging in too large a field of
inquiry, to attempt reasoning on the general lawfulness of slavery.
I trust, too, that the liberty, for which I am contending, doth not
require such a disquisition; and am impatient to reach that part of
my argument, in which I hope to prove slavery reprobated by the
law of England as an inconvenient thing. Here, therefore, I shall
only refer to some of the most eminent writers, who have examined
how far slavery founded on captivity or contract is conformable to
the law of nature, and shall just hint at the reasons, which influence
their several opinions. The ancient writers suppose the right of killing
an enemy vanquished in a just war; and thence infer the right of enslaving him. In this opinion founded, as I presume, on the idea of pun-
ishing the enemy for his injustice, they are followed by Albericus
Gentilis, Grotius, Pufendorf, Bynkershoek, and many others. But
in The Spirit of Laws the right of killing is denied, except in case
of absolute necessity and for self-preservation. However, where a
country is conquered, the author seems to admit the conqueror's
right of enslaving for a short time, that is, till the conquest is
effectually secured. Dr. Rutherforth, not satisfied with the right
of killing a vanquished enemy, infers the right of enslaving him, from
the conqueror's right to a reparation in damages for the expenses of
the war. I do not know that this doctrine has been examined; but
I must observe, that it seems only to warrant a temporary slavery,
till reparation is obtained from the property or personal labour of the
people conquered. The lawfulness of slavery by contract is assented
to by Grotius and Pufendorf, who found themselves on the
maintenance of the slave, which is the consideration moving from the
master. But a very great writer of our own country controverts
the sufficiency of such a consideration. Mr. Locke has framed
another kind of argument against slavery by contract; and the
substance of it is, that a right of preserving life is unalienable; that
freedom from arbitrary power is essential to the exercise of that right;
and, therefore, that no man can by compact enslave himself. Dr.
Rutherforth endeavours to answer Mr. Locke's objection, by

[margin] Origin of slavery, its general lawfulness considered.

insisting on various limitations to the despotism of the master; particularly, that he has no right to dispose of the slave's life at pleasure. But the misfortune of this reasoning is, that though the contract cannot justly convey an arbitrary power over the slave's life, it generally leaves him without a security against the exercise of that or any other power. I shall say nothing of slavery by birth; except that the slavery of the child must be unlawful, if that of the parent cannot be justified; and that when slavery is extended to the issue, as it usually is, it may be unlawful as to them, even though it is not so as to their parents. In respect to slavery used for the punishment of crimes against civil society, it is founded on the same necessity, as the right of inflicting other punishments; never extends to the offender's issue; and seldom is permitted to be domestic, the objects of it is being generally employed in public works, as the galley-slaves are in France. Consequently, this kind of slavery is not liable to the principal objections which occur against slavery in general. Upon the whole of this controversy concerning slavery, I think myself warranted in saying, that the justice and lawfulness of every species of it, as is generally constituted, except the limited one founded on the commission of crimes against civil society, is at least doubtful; that if in any case lawful, such circumstances are necessary to make it so, as seldom concur, and therefore render a just commencement of it barely possible; and that the oppressive manner in which it has generally commenced, the cruel means necessary to enforce its continuance, and the mischiefs ensuing from the permission of it, furnish very strong presumptions against its justice, and at all events evince the humanity and policy of those states, in which the use of it is no longer tolerated.

But however reasonable it may be to doubt the justice of domestic slavery, however convinced we may be of its ill effects, it must be confessed, that the practice is ancient and has been almost universal.

Universality of domestic slavery amongst the ancients. Its beginning may be dated from the remotest period, in which there are any traces of the history of mankind. It commenced in the barbarous state of society, and was retained, even when men were far advanced in civilization. The nations of antiquity most famous for countenancing the system of domestic slavery were the Jews, the Greeks, the Romans, and the ancient Germans; amongst all of whom it prevailed, but in various degrees of severity. By the ancient Germans it was continued in the countries they over-ran; and so was transmitted to the various kingdoms and states, which arose in Europe out of the ruins of the Roman Empire. At length, however, it fell into decline in most parts of Europe; and amongst the various causes which contributed to this alteration, none were Decline of probably more effectual than experience of the disadvantages of Slavery in Europe. slavery, the difficulty of continuing it, and a persuasion that the cruelty and oppression almost necessarily incident to it were irreconcileable with the pure morality of the Christian dispensation. The history of its decline in Europe has been traced by many eminent writers, particularly Bodin, Albericus Gentilis, Potgieserus, Dr. Robertson, and Mr. Millar. It is sufficient here to say that this great change began in Spain, according to Bodin, about the end of the eighth century, and was become general before the middle of the fourteenth century. Bartolus, the most famed commentator on the civil law in that period, represents slavery as in disuse; and the succeeding commentators hold much the same language. However, they must be understood with many restrictions and exceptions, and not to mean that slavery was completely and universally abolished in Europe. Some modern civilians, not sufficiently attending to this circumstance, rather too hastily reprehended their predecessors for representing slavery as disused in Europe. The truth is, that the ancient species of slavery by frequent emancipations became greatly diminished in extent; the remnant of it was considerably abated in severity; the disuse of the practice of enslaving captives taken in the wars between Christian powers assisting in preventing the future increase of domestic slavery; and in some countries of Europe, particularly England, a still more effectual method, which I shall explain hereafter, was thought of to perfect the suppression of it. Such was the expiring state of domestic slavery in Europe at the commencement of the sixteenth century, when the discovery of Revival of domestic America and of the western and eastern coasts of Africa gave slavery in America. occasion to the introduction of a new species of slavery. It took its rise from the Portuguese, who, in order to supply the Spaniards with persons able to sustain the fatigue of cultivating their new possessions in America, particularly the islands, opened a trade beeween Africa and America for the sale of negro slaves. This disgraceful commerce in the human species is said to have begun in the year 1508, when the first importation of negro slaves was made into Hispaniola from the Portuguese settlement on the western coasts of Africa. In 1540 the Emperor Charles V. endeavoured to stop the progress of the negro slavery, by orders that all slaves in the American isles should be made free, and they were accordingly manumitted by Lagasca, the governor of the country, on condition of continuing to labour for their masters. But this attempt proved unsuccessful, and on Lagasca's return to Spain domestic slavery revived and flourished as before. The expedient of having slaves for labour in America was not long peculiar to the Spaniards; being afterwards adopted by the other Europeans, as they acquired possessions there. In consequence of this general practice, negroes are become a very considerable article in the commerce between Africa and America; and domestic slavery has taken so deep a root in most of our own American colonies, as well as in those of other nations, that there is little probability of ever seeing it generally suppressed..

The attempt to introduce the slavery of negroes into England examined. — Here I conclude my observations on domestic slavery in general, I have exhibited a view of its nature, of its bad tendency, of its origin, of the arguments for and against its justice, of its decline in Europe, and the introduction of a new slavery by the European nations into their American colonies. I shall now examine the attempt to obtrude this new slavery into England. And here it will be material to observe, that if on the declension of slavery in this and other countries of Europe, where it is discountenanced, no means had been devised to obstruct the admission of a new slavery, it would have been vain and fruitless to have attempted superseding the ancient

Argument to prove that the law of England will not admit a new slavery. — species. But I hope to prove that our ancestors at least were not so short-sighted; and that long and uninterrupted usage has established rules, as effectual to prevent the revival of slavery, as their humanity was successful in once suppressing it. I shall endeavour to show that the law of England never recognised any species of domestic slavery, except the ancient one of villenage now expired, and has sufficiently provided against the introduction of a new slavery under the name of villenage or any other denomination whatever. This proposition I hope to demonstrate from the following considerations:

Argument from the manner of making title to a villein. — 1st. I apprehend that this will appear to be the law of England from the manner of making title to a villein.

The only slavery our law-books take the least notice of, is that of a villein; by whom was meant, not the mere tenant by villein services, who might be free in his person, but the villein in blood and tenure; and as the English law has no provisions to regulate any other slavery; therefore no slavery can be lawful in England, except such as will consistently fall under the denomination of villenage.

The condition of a villein. — The condition of a villein had most of the incidents which I have before described in giving the idea of slavery in general. His service was uncertain and indeterminate, such as his lord thought fit to require; or, as some of our ancient writers express it, he knew not in the evening what he was to do in the morning, he was bound to do whatever he was commanded. He was liable to beating, imprisonment, and every other chastisement his lord might prescribe, except killing and maiming. He was incapable of acquiring property for his own benefit, the rule being *quicquid acquiritur servo, acquiritur domino.* He was himself the subject of property; as such, saleable and transmissible. If he was a villein regardant, he passed with the manor or land to which he was annexed, but might be severed at the pleasure of his lord. If he was a villein in gross, he was an hereditament or a chattel real according to his lord's interest; being descendible to the heir where the lord was absolute owner, and transmissible to the executor where the lord had only a term of years in him. Lastly, the slavery extended to the issue, if both parents were villeins, or if the father only was a villein; our law deriving the condition of the child from that of the father, contrary to the Roman law, in which the rule was *partus sequitur ventrem.* The origin of villenage is principally to be derived from the wars between our British, Saxon, Danish, and Norman ancestors, whilst they were contending for the possession of this country. Judge Fitzherbert, in his reading on the 4 Edward I., Stat. I., entitled Extenta Manerii, supposes villenage to have commenced at the Conquest, by the distribution then made of the forfeited lands and of the vanquished inhabitants resident upon them. But there were many bondmen in England before the Conquest, as appears by the Anglo-Saxon laws regulating them; and, therefore, it would be nearer the truth to attribute the origin of villeins, as well to the preceding wars and revolutions in this country, as to the effects of the Conquest. *[margin: Origin of villenage.]*

After the Conquest many things happily concurred, first, to check the progress of domestic slavery in England, and, finally, to suppress it. The cruel custom of enslaving captives in war being abolished, from that time the accession of a new race of villeins was prevented, and the humanity, policy, and necessity of the times were continually wearing out the ancient race. Sometimes, no doubt, manumissions were freely granted; but they probably were much oftener extorted during the rage of the civil wars, so frequent before the reign of Henry VII., about the forms of the constitution or the succession to the crown. Another cause, which greatly contributed to the extinction of villenage was the discouragement of it by the courts of justice. They always presumed in favour of liberty, throwing the *onus probandi* upon the lord, as well in the writ of *homine replegiando,* where the villein was plaintiff, as in the *nativo habendo,* where he was defendant. *[margin: Decline of villenage.]*

Nonsuit of the lord after appearance in a *nativo habendo,* which was the writ for asserting the title of slavery, was a bar to another *nativo habendo,* and a perpetual enfranchisement; but nonsuit of the villein after appearance in a *libertate probando*, which was one of the writs for asserting the claim of liberty against the lord, was no bar to another writ of the like kind. If two plaintiffs joined in a *nativo habendo*, nonsuit of one was a nonsuit of both; but it was otherwise in a *libertate probando*. The lord could not prosecute for more than two villeins in one *nativo habendo*; but any number of villeins of the same blood might join in one *libertate probando*.

Manumissions were inferred from the slightest circumstances of mistake or negligence in the lord, from every act or omission which legal refinement could strain into an acknowledgment of the villein's liberty. If the lord vested the ownership of lands in the villein, received homage from him, or gave a bond to him, he was enfranchised. Suffering the vlllein to be on a jury, to enter into religion and be professed, or to stay a year and a day in ancient demesne without claim, were enfranchisements. Bringing ordinary actions against him, joining with him in actions, answering to his actions without protestation of villenage, imparling in them or assenting to his imparlance or suffering him to be vouched without counter-pleading the voucher, were also enfranchisements by implication of law. Most of the constructive manumissions I have mentioned were the received law, even in the reign of the first Edward. I have been the more particular in enumerating these instances of extraordinary favour to liberty : because the anxiety of our ancestors to emancipate the ancient villeins well accounts for the establishment of any rules of law calculated to obstruct the introduction of a new stock. It was natural that the same opinions, which influenced to discountenance the former, should lead to the prevention of the latter.

When villenage expired.

I shall not attempt to follow villenage in the several stages of its decline, it being sufficient here to mention the time of its extinction, which, as all agree, happened about the latter end of Elizabeth's reign or soon after the accession of James. One of the last instances in which villenage was insisted upon, was *Crouch's case*, reported in Dyer and other books. An entry having been made by one Butler on some lands purchased by Crouch, the question was, whether he was Butler's *villein regardant* ; and on two special verdicts, the one in ejectment Mich. 9th and 10th Eliz., and the other in Assizes Easter 11th Eliz., the claim of villenage was disallowed, one of the reasons given for the judgment in both being the want of seizin of the villein's person within 60 years, which is the time limited by the 32rd of Hen. 8, chap. 2, in all cases of hereditaments claimed by prescription. This is generally said to have been the case of villenage ; but there are four subsequent cases in print. One was in

Hilary 18th of Eliz.; another was a judgment in Easter, 1st of James; the third, which was never determined, happened in Trinity 8th James, and the fourth was so late as Hilary 15th James. From the 15th of James I, being more than 150 years ago, the claim of villenage has not been heard of in our courts of justice; and nothing can be more notorious, than that the race of persons who were once the objects of it was, about that time, completely worn out by the continual and united operation of deaths and manumissions.

But though villenage itself is obsolete, yet fortunately those rules, by which the claim of it was regulated, are not yet buried in oblivion. These the industry of our ancestors has transmitted; nor let us, their posterity, despise the reverend legacy. By a strange progress of human affairs, the memory of slavery expired now furnishes one of the chief obstacles to the introduction of slavery attempted to be revived; and the venerable reliques of the learning relative to villenage, so long consigned to gratify the investigating curiosity of the antiquary, or used as a splendid appendage to the ornaments of the scholar, must now be drawn forth from their faithful repositories for a more noble purpose; to inform and guide the sober judgment of this court, and, as I trust, to preserve this country from the miseries of domestic slavery.

Littleton says every villein is either a villein by title of prescription, to wit, that he and his ancestors have been villeins time out of memory, or he is a villein by his own confession in a court of record. And in another place his description of a villein regardant and of a villein in gross shows that title cannot be made to either without prescription or confession. Time whereof no memory runs to the contrary is an inseparable incident to every prescription, and therefore, according to Littleton's account of villenage, the lord must prove the slavery ancient and immemorial, or the villein must solemnly confess it to be so in a court of justice. A still earlier writer lays down the rule in terms equally strong. No one, says Britton, can be a villein except of ancient nativity, or by acknowledgment. All the proceedings in cases of villenage, when contested, conform to this idea of remote antiquity in the slavery, and are quite irreconcileable with one of modern commencement.

Manner of making title to a villein.

1. The villein in all such suits between him and his lord was styled *nativus* as well as *villanus;* our ancient writers describe a female slave by no other name than that of *neif;* and the technical name of the only writ in the law for the recovery of a villein is equally remarkable, being always called the *nativo habendo*, or writ of neifty.

This peculiarity of denomination, which implies that villenage is a slavery by birth, might perhaps of itself be deemed too slight a fonndation for any solid argument; but when combined with other circumstances more decisive, it is not without very considerable force.

2. In pleading villenage where it had not been confessed on some former occasion, the lord always founded his title on prescription. Our Year Books, and books of entries, are full of the forms used in pleading a title to villeins regardant. In the *homine replegiando*, and other actions where the plea of villenage was for the purpose of showing the plaintiff's disability to sue, if the villein was regardant, the defendant alleged, that he was seised of such a manor, and that the plaintiff and his ancestors had been villeins belonging to the manor time out of mind, and that the defendant and his ancestors and all those whose estate he had in the manor had been seised of the plaintiff and all his ancestors as of villeins belonging to it. In the *nativo habendo* the form of making title to a villein regardant was in substance the same. In fact, regardancy necessarily implies prescription, being where one and his ancestors have been annexed to a manor time out of the memory of man. As to villeins in gross, the cases relative to them are very few; and I am inclined to think, that there never was any great number of them in England. The author of the Mirror, who wrote in the reign of Edward II., only mentions villeins regardant; and Sir Thomas Smith, who was secretary of state in the reign of Edward VI.. says, that in his time he never knew a villein in gross throughout the realm. However, after a long search, I do find places in the Year Books, where the form of alleging villenage in gross is expressed, not in full terms, but in a general way ; and in all cases I have yet seen, the villenage is alleged in the ancestor of the person against whom it was pleaded, and in one of these the words " time beyond memory " are added. But if precedents had been wanting the authority of Littleton, according to whom the title to villenage of each kind, unless it has been confessed, must be by prescription, would not have left the least room for supposing the pleading of a prescription less necessary on the claim of villeins in gross than of those regardant.

3. The kind of evidence which the law required to proved villenage, and allowed in disproof of it, is only applicable to a slavery in blood and family, one uninterruptedly transmitted through a long line of ancestors to the person against whom it was alleged. On the lord's part, it was necessary that he should prove the slavery against his villein by other villeins of the same blood, such as were descended from the same common male stock, and would acknowledge themselves

villeins to the lord, or those from whom he derived his title; and at least two witnesses of this description were requisite for the purpose. Nay, so strict was the law in this respect, that in the *nativo habendo* the defendant was not obliged to plead to the claim of villenage, unless the lord, at the time of declaring on his title, brought his witnesses with him into court, and they acknowledged themselves villeins, and swore to their consanguinity with the defendant; and if the plaintiff failed in adducing such previous evidence, the judgment of the court was, that the defendant should be free for ever, and the plaintiff was amerced for his false claim. In other actions, the production of suit or witnesses by the plaintiff, previously to the defendant's pleading, fell into disuse some time in the reign of Edward III ; and ever since, the entry of such production on the rolls of the court has been mere form, being always with an &c., and without naming the witnesses. But in the *nativo habendo* the actual production of the suit, and also the examination of them, unless the defendant released it in court, continued to be indispensable even down to the time when villenage expired. Such was the sort of testimony by which only the lord could support the title of slavery: nor were the means of defence on the part of the villein less remarkable. If he could prove that the slavery was not in his blood and family, he entitled himself to liberty. The author of the *Mirror* expressly says, that a proof of a free stock was an effectual defence against the claims of villenage; and even, in the time of Henry the Second, the law of England was in this respect, the same, as appears by the words of Glanville. In his chapter of the trial of liberty, he says, that the person claiming it shall produce "*plures de proximis et consanguineis de eodem stipite unde ipse exierat exeuntes; per puorum libertates, si fuerint in curia recognitæ et probatæ, liberabitur a jugo servitutis qui ad libertatem proclamatur.*" But the special defences which the law permitted against villenage, are still more observable; and prove it beyond a contradiction to be what the author of the *Mirror* emphatically styles it, a slavery of so great an antiquity that no free stock can be found by human remembrance. Whenever the lord sued to recover a villein by a *nativo habendo,* or alleged villenage in other actions as a disability to sue, the person claimed as a villein might either plead generally that he was of free condition, and on the trial of this general issue, avail himself of every kind of defence which the law permits against villenage; or he might plead specially any single fact or thing, which, if true, was of itself a legal bar to the claim of villenage; and, in that case, the lord was compellable to answer the special matter. Of this special kind, were the pleas of bastardy and adventif. The

former was an allegation by the supposed villein, that either himsel
or his father, grandfather, or other male ancestor, was born out of
matrimony; and this plea, however remote the ancestor in whom the
bastardy was alleged, was peremptory to the lord; that is, if true, it
destroyed the claim of villenage, and therefore the lord could only
support his title by denying the fact of bastardy. This appears to
have been the law from a great variety of the most ancient authorities.
The first of them is a determined case, so early as the 13th of Edward
the Second; and in all the subsequent cases, the doctrine is received
for law without once being drawn into question. In one of them,
the reason why bastardy is a good plea in a bar, against villenage, is
expressed in a very peculiar manner; for the words of the book are,
"When one claims any man as his villein, it shall be intended always
that he is his villein, by reason of stock; and this is the reason that
there shall be an answer to the special matter, when he alleges
bastardy, because, if his ancestor was a bastard, he can never be a
villein, unless by subsequent acknowledgment in a court of record."
The force of this reason will appear fully on recollection, that the
law of England always derives the condition of the issue from that of
the father, and the father of a bastard being, in law, uncertain, it
was, therefore, impossible to prove a bastard a slave by descent. In
respect to the plea of adventif, there is some little confusion in the
explanation our Year Books give us of the persons to whom the
description of adventif is applicable; but the form of the plea will
best show the precise meaning of it. It alleged, that either the
person himself who was claimed as a villein regardant to a manor, or
one of his ancestors, was born in a county different from that in
which the manor was, and so was free, which was held to be a
necessary conclusion to the plea. This in general was the form of
the plea, but sometimes it was more particular, as in the following
case:—In trespass, the defendant pleads that the plaintiff is his
vellein regardant to his manor of Dale; the plaintiff replies, that his
great-grandfather was born in C., in the county of N., and from thence
went into the county of S., and took lands held in bondage within the
manor to which the plaintiff is supposed to be a villein regardant, and
so after time of memory his great-grandfather was adventif. It is plain
from this case, that the plea of adventif was calculated to destroy the
claim to villenage regardant, by showing that the connection of the
supposed villein and his ancestors with the manner to which they
were supposed to be regardant, had begun within time of memory;
and as holding land by villein-services was anciently deemed a mark,
though not a certain one, of personal bondage, I conjecture that

this special matter was never pleaded, except to distinguish the mere tenant by villein-services from the villein in blood as well as tenure· But whatever might be the cases proper for the plea of adventif, it is one other incontrovertible proof, in addition to the proofs already mentioned, that no slavery having had commencement within time of memory was lawful in England; and that if one ancestor could be found whose blood was untarnished with the stain of slavery, the title of villenage was no longer capable of being sustained.

Such were the striking peculiarities in the manner of making title to a villein, and of contesting the question of liberty; and it is scarce possible to attend to the enumeration of them, without anticipating the inferences I have to make. The law of England only knows slavery by birth; it requires prescription in making title to a slave; it receives on the lord's part no testimony except such as proves the slavery to have been always in the blood and family, on the villein's part every testimony which proves the slavery to have been once out of his blood and family, it allows nothing to sustain the slavery except what shows its commencement beyond the time of memory; every thing to defeat the slavery which evinces its commencement within the time of memory. But in our American colonies and other conntries slavery may be by captivity or contract as well as by birth; no prescription is requisite; nor is it necessary that slavery should be in the blood and family, and immemorial. Therefore the law of England is not applicable to the slavery of our American colonies, or of other countries. If the law of England would permit the introduction of a slavery commencing out of England, the rules it prescribes for trying the title to a slave would be applicable to such a slavery; but they are not so; and from thence it is evident that the introduction of such a slavery is not permitted by the law of England. The law of England, then, excludes every slavery not commencing in England, every slavery though commencing there not being ancient and immemorial. Villenage is the only slavery which can possibly answer to such a description, and that has long expired by the deaths and emancipations of all those who were once the objects of it. Consequently there is now no slavery which can be lawful in England, until the legislature shall interpose its authority to make it so.

This is plain, and unadorned, and direct reasoning; it wants no aid from the colours of art, or the embellishments of language; it is composed of necessary inferences from facts and rules of law, which do not admit of contradiction; and I think, that it must be vain

[Marginal note: How it is that the rules of law concerning villenage exclude a new slavery.]

to attempt shaking a superstructure raised on such solid foundations.

As to the other arguments I have to adduce against the revival of domestic slavery, I do confess that they are less powerful, being merely presumptive. But then I must add, that they are strong and violent presumptions; such as furnish more certain grounds of judicial decision than are to be had in many of the cases which become the subjects of legal controversy. For—

2ndly. I infer the law of England will not permit a new slavery, from the fact of there never yet having been any slavery but villenage, and from the actual extinction of that ancient slavery. If a new slavery could have lawfully commenced here, or lawfully have been introduced from a foreign country, is there the most remote proba bility, that in the course of so many centuries a new slavery should never have arisen? If a new race of slaves could have been introduced under the denomination of villeins—if a new slavery could have been from time to time engrafted on the ancient stock, would the laws of villenage have once become obsolete for want of objects, or would not a successive supply of slaves have continued their operation to the present times? But, notwithstanding the vast extent of our commercial connections, the fact is confessedly otherwise. The ancient slavery has once expired; neither natives nor foreigners have yet succeeded in the introduction of a new slavery; and from thence the strongest presumption arises, that the law of England does not permit such an introduction.

Argument slavery from the rules of law against slavery by contract.

3rdly. I insist, that the unlawfulness of introducing a new slavery into England, from our American colonies or any other country, is deducible from the rules of the English law concerning contracts of service. The law of England will not permit any man to enslave himself by contract. The utmost, which our law allows. is a contract to serve for life; and some perhaps may even doubt the validity of such a contract, there being no detetmined cases directly affirming its lawfulness. In the reign of Henry the fourth there is a case of debt, brought by a servant against the master's executors, on a retainer to serve for term or life in peace and war for one hundred shillings a year; but it was held that debt did not lie for want of a speciality; which, as was agreed, would not have been necessary in the case of a common labourer's salary, because, as the case is explained by Brooke in abridging it, the latter is bound to serve by statute. This case is the only one I can find, in which a contract to serve for life is mentioned, and even in this case there is no judicial decision on the force of it. Nor did the nature of the case require any opinion upon such a contract; the action not being to establish the contract against the servant, but to enforce payment against the master's executors for arrears of salary in respect of service actually performed; and therefore this case will scarce bear any interference in favour of a contract to serve for life. Certain also it is, that a service for life in England is not usual, except in the case of a military person; whose service, though in effect for life, is rather so by the operation of the yearly acts for regulating the army, and of the perpetual act for governing the navy, than in consequence of any express agreement. However, I do not mean absolutely to deny the lawfulness of agreeing to serve for life; nor will the inferences I shall draw from the rules of law concerning servitude by contract be in the least affected by admitting such agreements to be lawful. The law of England may perhaps give effect to a contract of service for life; but that is the *ne plus ultra* of servitude by contract in England. It will not allow the servant to invest the master with an arbitrary power of correcting, imprisoning, or alienating him; it will not permit him to renounce the capacity of acquiring and enjoying property, or to transmit a contract of service to his issue. In other words, it will not permit him to incorporate into his contract the ingredients of slavery. And why is it that the law of England rejects a contract of slavery? The only reason to be assigned is, that the law of England, acknowledging only the ancient slavery which is now expired, will not allow the introduction of a new species, even though founded on consent of the party. The same reason operates with double force against a new slavery founded on captivity in war, and introduced from another country. Will the law of England condemn a new slavery commencing by consent of the party, and at the same time approve of one founded on force, and most probably on oppression also? Will the law of England invalidate a new slavery commencing in this country, when the title to the slavery may be fairly examined, and at the same time give effect to a new slavery introduced from another country, when disproof of the slavery must generally be impossible? This would be rejecting and receiving a new slavery at the same moment, rejecting slavery the least odious, receiving slavery the most odious: and by such an inconsistency, the wisdom and justice of the English law would be completely dishonoured. Nor will this reasoning be weakened by observing that our law permitted villenage, which was a slavery confessed to originate from force and captivity in war, because that was a slavery coeval with the first formation of the English constitution, and consequently had a commencement here prior to the establishment of those rules which the common law furnishes against slavery by contract.

Having thus explained the three great arguments which I oppose
to the introduction of domestic slavery from our American colonies,
or any foreign country, it is now proper to inquire, how far the subject is affected by the cases and judicial decisions since or just before
the extinction of villenage.

The first case on the subject is mentioned in Mr. Rushworth's
Historical Collections ; where it is said, that in the 11th year of
Queen Elizabeth, one Cartwright brought a slave from Russia, and
would scourge him ; for which he was questioned ; and it was resolved, that England was too pure an air for a slave to breathe in.
In order to judge what degree of credit is due to the representation
of this case, it will be proper to state from whom Mr. Rushworth
reports it. In 1637, there was a proceeding by information in the
Star-Chamber against the famous John Lilburne, for printing and
publishing a libel ; and for his contempt in refusing to answer inter
rogatories, he was by order of the court imprisoned till he should
answer, and also whipped, pilloried, and fined. His imprisonment
continued till 1640, when the Long Parliament began. He was
then released, and the House of Commons impeached the judges of
the Star-Chamber for their proceedings against Lilburne. In speaking to this impeachment, the managers of the Commons cited the
case of the Russian slave. Therefore the truth of the case does not
depend upon John Lilburne's assertion, as the learned observer on
the ancient statutes seems to apprehend ; but rests upon the credit
due to the managers of the Commons. When this is considered,
and that the year of the reign in which the case happened is mentioned, with the name of the person who brought the slave into
England ; that not above seventy-two or seventy three years had
intervened between the fact and the relation of it ; and also that the
case could not be supposed to have any influence on the fate of the
impeachment against the judges ; I see no great objection to a
belief of the case. If the account of it is true, the plain inference
from it is, that the slave was become free by his arrival in England.
Any other construction renders the case unintelligible, because
scourging, or even correction of a severer kind, was allowed by the
law of England to the lord in the punishment of his villein ; and
consequently, if our law had recognised the Russian slave, his master
would have been justified in scourging him.

The first case in our printed Reports is, that of Butts against
Penny, which is said to have been adjudged by the Court of King's
Bench in Trinity term, 29th of Charles the 2nd. It was an action
of trover for ten negroes, and there was a special verdict—finding

that the negroes were infidels, subjects to an infidel prince, and usually bought and sold in India as merchandise, by the custom, amongst merchants, and that the plaintiff had bought them, and was in possession of them, and that the defendant took them out of his possession. The Court held, that negroes being usually bought and sold amongst merchants in India, and being infidels, there might be a property in them sufficient to maintain the action: and it is said that judgment nisi was given for the plaintiff, but that on the prayer of the counsel for the defendant, to be further heard in the case, time was given till the next term. In this way, our reporters state the case: and if nothing further appeared, it might be cited as an authority, though a very feeble one, to shew that the master's property in his negro slaves, continues after their arrival in England, and consequently that the negroes are not emancipated by being brought here. But having a suspicion of some defect in the state of the case, I desired an examination of the Roll: and according to the account of it given to me, though the declaration is for negroes generally in London, without any mention of foreign parts, yet from the special verdict it appears, that the action was really brought to recover the value of negroes, of which the plaintiff had been possessed, not in England, but in India. Therefore, this case would prove nothing in favour of slavery in England, even if it had received the Court's judgment, which, however, it never did receive—there being only an "*ulterius consilium*" on the Roll.

The next case of trover was between Gelly and Cleve, in the Common Pleas, and was adjudged in Michaelmas term, 5th of William and Mary. In the report of this case, the Court is said to have been held—that trover will lie for a negro boy, because negroes are heathens: and therefore a man may have property in them, and the Court, without averment, will take notice that they are heathens. On examination of the Roll, I find that the action was brought for various articles of merchandize, as well as the negro: and I suspect, that in this case, as well as the former one of Butts and Penny, the action was for a negro in America: but the declaration being laid generally, and there being no special verdict, it is now too late to ascertain the fact. I will therefore suppose the action to have been for a negro in England, and admit that it tends to shew the lawfulness of having negro-slaves in England. But then, if the case is to be understood in this sense, I say that it appears to have been adjudged without solemn argument: that there is no reasoning in the report of this case, to impeach the principles of law on which I have argued against the revival of slavery in England: that unless those

principles can be controverted with success, it will be impossible to
sustain the authority of such a case: and further, that it stands contradicted by a subsequent case: in which the question of slavery
came directly before the Court.

The only other reported case of trover, is that of Smith against
Gould, which was adjudged, Mich. 4 Ann, in the King's Bench.
The trover, for several things, and, among the rest, for a negro, not
guilty, was pleaded, and there was a verdict for the plaintiff, with
several damages, £30 being given for the negro : and after argument
on a motion, in arrest of judgment, the Court held that trover did
not lie for a negro. If in this case the action was for a negro in
England, the judgment in it is a direct contradiction to the case of
Gelly and Cleve. But I am inclined to think, that in this, as well as
in the former cases of trover, the negroes for which the actions were
brought, were not in England : and that in all of them, the question
was not on the lawfulness of having negro-slaves in England: but
merely whether trover was the proper kind of action for recovering
the value of a negro unlawfully detained from the owner in America
and India. The things, for which trover in general lies, are those in
which the owner has an absolute property, without limitation in the
use of them: whereas, the master's power over the slave doth not
extend to his life, and consequently, the master's property in the
slave is, in some degree, qualified and limited. Supposing, therefore,
the cases of trover to have been determined on this distinction, I
will not insist upon any present benefit from them in argument
though the last of them, if it will bear any material inference, is
certainly an authority against slavery in England.

The next cases I shall state, is a judgment by the King's Bench
in Hilary 8th and 9th of William the III. Trespass *vi et armis* was
thought by Chamberlain against Harvey, for taking a negro of the
value of £160 : and by the special verdict, it appears that the negro,
for which the plaintiff sued, had been brought from Barbadoes into
England, and was here baptized without the plaintiff's consent
and at the time when the trespass was alleged, was in the
defendant's service, and had £6 a-year for wages. In the argument of this case, three questions were made. One was, whether
the facts in the verdict sufficiently shewed that the plaintiff had
even had a vested property in the negro: another was, whether
that property was not divested by bringing the negro into England:
and the third was, whether trespass for taking a man of the value
of £100, was the proper action. After several arguments, the
Court gave judgment against the plaintiff. But I do confess,

that in the reports we have of the cases, no opinion on the great question of slavery is mentioned: it becoming unnecessary to declare one, as the Court held, that the action should have been an action to recover damages for the loss of the services, and not to recover the value of the slave. Of this case, therefore, I shall not attempt to avail myself. But the next case, which was an action of *Indebitatus Assumpsit* in the King's Bench, by Smith, against Browne and Cooper, is more to the purpose The plaintiff declared for £20 for a negro sold by him to the defendants in London, and on motion in arrest of judgmeut, the court held that the plaintiff should have averred in the declaration, that the negro at the time of he sale was in Virginia, and that negroes by the laws and statutes of Virginia are saleable. In these words there is a direct opinion against the slavery of negroes in England: for if it was lawful, the negro would have been saleable and transferable here, as well as in Virginia; and stating, that the negro at the time of the sale was in Virginia, could not have been essential to the sufficiency of the declaration. But the influence of this case, on the question of slavery, is not by mere inference from the court's opinion on the plaintiff's mode of declaring in his action. The language of the judges, in giving that opinion, is remarkably strong against the slavery of negroes, and every other new slavery attempted to be introduced into Englaud. Mr. Justice Powell says, " In a villein the owner has a property; the villein is an inheritance, but the law takes no notice of a negro." Lord Chief Justice Holt is still more explicit; for he says, that "one may be a villein in England;" but that "as soon as a negro comes into England, he becomes free." The words of these two great judges contain the whole of the proposition, for which I am contending. They admit property in the villein; they deny property in the negro. They assent to the old slavery of the villein; they disallow the new slavery of the negro.

I beg leave to mention one other case, chiefly for the sake of introducing a strong expression of the late Lord Chancellor Northington. It is the case of Shanley v. Hervey, which was determined in Chancery some time in March, 1762. Iu Shanley v. Hervey the question was between a negro and his former master, who claimed the benefit of a *donatio mortis causa* made to the negro by a lady, on whom he had attended as servant for several years by the permission of his master. Lord Northington disallowed the master's claim, and gave the costs to the negro. He said, "As soon as a man sets his foot on English ground, he is free; a negro may maintain an action against his master for ill usage, and may have a *habeas corpus*, if restrained of his liberty."

Objections
stated and
answered.

Having observed upon cases, in which there is anything to be found relative to the present lawfulness of slavery in England, it is time to consider the force of the several objections, which are likely to be made, as well to the inferences I have drawn from the determined cases, as to the general doctrine I have been urging.

1. It may be asked, why it is that the law should permit the ancient slavery of the villein, and yet disallow a slavery of modern commencement ?

To this I answer, that villenage sprung up amongst our ancestors in the early and barbarous state of society, that afterwards more humane customs and wiser opinions prevailed, and by their influence rules were established for checking the progress of slavery, and that it was thought most prudent to effect this great object, not instantaneously by declaring every slavery unlawful, but gradually by excluding a new race of slaves, and encouraging the voluntary emancipation of the ancient race. It might have seemed an arbitrary exertion of power, by a retrospective law to have annihilated property, which, however inconvenient, was already vested, under the sanction of existing laws, by lawful means; but it was policy without injustice to restrain future acquisitions.

2. It may be said, that as there is nothing to hinder persons of free condition from becoming slaves by acknowledging themselves to be villeins, therefore a new slavery is not contrary to law.

The force of this objection arises from a supposition, that confession or acknowledgment of villenage is a legal mode of creating slavery; but, on examining the nature of the acknowledgment, it will be evident, that the law does not permit villenage to be acknowledged for any such purpose. The term itself imports something widely different from creation; the acknowledgment, or confession of a thing, implying that the thing acknowledged or confessed has a previous existence, and in all cases, criminal as well as civil, the law intends, that no man will confess an untruth to his own disadvantage, and therefore never requires proof of that which is admitted to be true by the person interested to deny it. Besides, it is not allowable to institute a proceeding for the avowed and direct purpose of acknowledging villenage, for the law would not allow the confession of it to be received, except whose villenage is alleged in an adverse way that is, only when villenage was pleaded by the lord against one whom he claimed as his villein, or by the villein against strangers, in order to excuse himself from defending actions to which his lord only was the proper party; or when one villein was produced to prove villenage against another of the same blood who denied the slavery. If the acknowledgment had been permitted as a creation of slavery would the law have required that the confession should be made in a mode so indirect and circuitous as a suit professedly commenced for a different purpose? If confession is a creation of slavery, it certainly must be deemed a creation by consent, but if confession had been adopted as a voluntary creation of slavery, would the law have restrained the courts of justice from receiving confession, except in an adverse way? If confession had been allowed as a mode of creating slavery, would the law have received the confession of one person as good evidence of slavery in another of the same blood merely because they were descended from the same common ancestor? This last circumstance is of itself decisive, because it necessarily implied, that a slavery confessed was a slavery by descent.

On a consideration of these circumstances attending the acknowledgment of villenage, I think it impossible to doubt its being merely a confession of that antiquity in the slavery, which was otherwise necessary to be proved. But if a doubt can be entertained, the opinions of the greatest lawyers may be produced to remove it, and to show, that, in consideration of law, the person confessing was a villein by descent and in blood.

In the Year Book of 43 George III., it is laid down as a general rule, "That when one claims any man as his villein, it shall be intended always that he is his villein by reason of stock." Lord Chief Justice Hobart considers villenage by confession, in this way, and says, "The confession in the Court of Record, is not so much a creation, as it is in supposal of law a declaration of rightful villenage before, as a confession in other actions." Mr. Sergeant Rolle too, in his abridgment, when he is writing on villenage by acknowledgment, uses very strong words to the same effect. He says, in one place, "It seems intended that title is made by prescription, wherefore the issue should also be villeins." The only instance I can find, of a Native Hatendo, founded on a previous acknowledgment of villenage, is a strong authority to the same purpose. In the 19th of Edward II., the dean and chapter of London brought a writ of guilty to recover a villein, and concluded their declaration with mentioning his acknowledgment of the villenage on a former occasion, instead of producing their suit, or witnesses, as was necessary when the villenage had not been confessed: but notwithstanding the acknowledgment, the plaintiffs alleged a seizin of the villein with *esplees,* or receipt of profits from him, in the usual manner. This case is another proof, that a seizin previous to the acknowledgment, was the real foundation of the lord's claim, and that the acknowledgment was merely used to stop the villein from contesting a fact which had been before solemnly confessed. However, I do admit, that under the form of acknowledgment, there was a possibility of collusively creating slavery. But this was not practicable without the concurrence of the person himself who was to be the sufferer by the fraud; and it was not probable that many persons should be found so base in mind, so false to themselves, as to sell themselves and their posterity, and to renounce the common protection and benefit of the law for a bare maintenance, which, by the wise provision of the law in this country, may always be had by the most needy and distressed, on terms infinitely less ignoble and severe. It should also be remembered, and such a collusion could scarcely be wholly prevented, so long as any of the real and unmanumitted descendants from the ancient villeins remained: because these would have been the same possibility of defrauding the law on the actual trial of villenage, as by a previous acknowledgment. Besides, if collusions of this sort had ever become frequent, the legislature might have prevented their effect by an extraordinary remedy. It seems that anciently, such frauds were sometimes practised: and that free persons, in order to evade the trial of actions brought against them, alleged that they were villeins to a stranger to the suit, which, on account of the great improbability that a confession so disadvantageous should be void of truth, was a plea the common law did not suffer the plaintiff to deny. But a remedy was soon applied, and the statute of 37 George III. was made—giving to the plaintiff a liberty of contesting such an allegation of villenage. If, in these times, it should be endeavoured to revive domestic slavery in England, by a like fraudulent confession of villenage, surely so unworthy an attempt, so gross an evasion of the law, would excite in this Court the strongest disapprobation and resentment, and from Parliament would receive an immediate and effectual remedy: I mean, a law, declaring that villenage, as is most notoriously the fact, has been long expired for want of real objects, and therefore making void all precedent confessions of it, and prohibiting the Courts of Justice from recording a confession of villenage in future.

3. It may be objected, that though it is not usual in the wars between Christian powers to enslave prisoners, yet some nations, particularly the several states on the coast of Barbary, still adhere to that inhuman practice; that in case of our being at war with

them, the law of nations would justify our king in retaliating; and consequently, that the law of England has not excluded the possibility of introducing a new slavery, as the arguments against it suppose.

But this objection may be easily answered; for if the arguments against a new slavery in England, are well founded, they reach the king, as well as his subjects. If it has been at all times the policy of the law of England not to recognise any slavery but the ancient one of the villein, which is now expired: we cannot consistently attribute to the executive power a prerogative of rendering that policy ineffectual. It is true, that the law of nations may give a right of retaliating on an enemy who enslaves his captives in war; but then the exercise of this right may be prevented or limited by the law of any particular country. A writer of eminence, on the law of nations, has a passage very applicable to this subject. His words are, "If the civil law of any nation does not allow of slavery, prisoners of war, who are taken by that nation, cannot be made slaves." He is justified in his observation, not only by the reason of the thing, but by the practices of some nations, where slavery is as unlawful as it is in England. The Dutch, when at war with the Algerines, Tunisians, or Tripolitans, make no scruple of retaliating on their enemies; but slavery not being lawful in their European dominions, they have usually sold their prisoners of war as slaves in Spain, where slavery is still permitted. To this example, I have only to add, that I do not know an instance, in which a prerogative of having captive slaves in England, has been assumed by the Crown; and it being also the policy of our law not to admit a new slavery, there appears neither reason nor fact, to suppose the existence of a royal prerogative to introduce it.

4. Another objection will be, that there are English Acts o Parliament, which give a sanction to the slavery of negroes; and therefore that it is now lawful, whatever it might be antecedently to those statutes.

The statutes in favour of this objection, are 5 George II., cap. 7, which makes negroes in America liable to all debts, simple-contract, as well as speciality; and the statutes regulating the African trade, particularly the 32 George II., cap. 31, which in the preamble recites, that the trade to Africa is advantageous to Great Britain, and necessary for supplying its colonies with negroes.

But the utmost which can be said of these statutes is, that they impliedly authorise the slavery of negroes in America; and it would be a strange thing to say, that permitting slavery there, includes a permission of slavery here. By an unhappy concurrence of circumstances, the slavery of negroes is thought to have become necessary in America; and therefore in America, our legislature has permitted the slavery of negroes. But the slavery of negroes is unnecessary in England, and therefore the legislature has not extended the permission of it to England; and not having done so, how can this court be warranted to make such an extension?

5. The slavery of negroes being admitted to be lawful now in America, however questionable its first introduction there might be, it may be urged, that the *lex loci* ought to prevail, and that the master's property in the negro as a slave, having had a lawful commencement in America, cannot be justly varied by bringing him into England.

I shall answer this objection by explaining the limitation under which the *lex loci* ought always to be received. It is a general rule that the *lex loci* shall not prevail, if great inconveniences will ensue from giving effect to it. Now I apprehend that no instance can be mentioned, in which an application of the *lex loci* would be more inconvenient than in the case of slavery. It must be agreed, that where the *lex loci* cannot have effect without introducing the thing prohibited in a degree either as great, or nearly as great, as if there was no prohibition, there the greatest inconvenience would ensue from regarding the *lex loci*, and consequently it ought not to prevail. Indeed, by receiving it under such circumstances, the end of a prohibition would be frustrated, either entirely or in a very great degree; and so the prohibition of things the most pernicious in their tendency would become vain and fruitless. At what greater inconveniences can we imagine than those which would necessarily result from such an unlimited sacrifice of the municipal law to the law of a foreign country? I will now apply this general doctrine to the particular case of our own law concerning slavery. Our law prohibits the commencement of domestic slavery in England; because it disapproves of slavery, and considers its operation as dangerous and destructive to the whole community. But would not this prohibition be wholly ineffectual, if slavery could be introduced from a foreign country? In the course of time, though perhaps in a progress less rapid, would not domestic slavery become as general, and be as completely revived in England by introduction from our colonies and from foreign countries, as if it was permitted to revive by commencement here; and would not the same inconveniences follow? To prevent the revival of domestic slavery effectually, its introduction must be resisted universally, without regard to the place of its commencement, and therefore, in the instance of slavery, the *lex loci* must yield to the municipal law. From the fact of there never yet having been any slavery in this country, except the old and now expired one of villenage, it is evident that hitherto our law has uniformly controlled the *lex loci* in this respect; and so long as the same policy of excluding slavery is retained by the law of England, it must continue entitled to the same preference. Nor let it be thought a peculiar want of complaisance in the law of England, that, disregarding the *lex loci* in the case of slaves, it gives immediate and entire liberty to them when they are brought here from another country. Most of the other European states, in which slavery is discountenanced, have adopted a like policy.

In Scotland domestic slavery is unknown, except so far as regards the coal-hewers and salt-makers, whose condition, it must be confessed, bears some resemblance to slavery; because all who have once acted in either of these capacities are compellable to serve, and fixed to their respective places of employment for life. But with this single exception—there is not the least vestige of slavery, and so jealous is the Scotch law of everything tending to slavery, that it has been held to disallow contracts of service for life, or for a very long term: as, for sixty years. However, no particular case has yet happened, in which it has been necessary to decide, whether a slave of another country acquires freedom on his arrival in Scotland. In 1757 this question was depending in the Court of Session, in the case of a negro, but the negro happening to die during the pendency of the cause, the question was not determined. But when it is considered, that in the time of Sir Thomas Craig, who wrote at least 150 years ago, slavery was even then a thing unheard of in Scotland, and that there are no laws to regulate slavery, one can scarce doubt what opinion the lords of session would have pronounced, if the negro's death had not prevented a decision.

In the United Provinces, slavery having fallen into disuse, all their writers agree, that slaves from another country become free the moment they enter into the Dutch territories. The same custom prevails in some of the neighbouring countries, particularly Brabant, and other parts of the Austrian Netherlands; and Gudelinus, an eminent civilian, who was formerly professor of law at Louvain in Brabant, relates from the annals of the supreme council at Mechlin, that, in the year 1531 an application for apprehending and surrendering a fugitive slave from Spain, was on this account rejected.

In France the law is particularly explicit against regarding the *lex loci* in the case of domestic slavery, and though in some of the provinces, a remnant of the ancient slavery is still to be seen in the persons of the "serfs," or 'gens de main-morte,' who are attached to particular lands as villeins regardant formerly were in England. Yet all the writers on the law of France agree, that the moment a slave arrives there from another country, he acquires liberty, not in consequence of any written law, but merely by long usuage having the force of law. There are many remarkable instances in which this rule against the admission of slaves from foreign countries has had effect in France. Two are mentioned by Bodin; one being the case of a foreign merchant who had purchased a slave in Spain, and after. wards carried him into France; the other being the case of a Spanish ambassador, whose slave was declared free, notwithstanding the high and independent character of the slave's owner. This latter case has been objected to by some writers on the laws of nations, who do not disapprove of the general principle on which liberty is given to slaves brought from foreign countries, but only complain of its application to the particular case of an ambassador. But, on the other hand, Wicquefort blames the states of Holland for not following the example of the French, in a case which he mentions. After the establishment of the French colónies in South America, the Kings of France thought fit to deviate from the strictness of the ancient French law, in respect to slavery, and in them to permit and regulate the possession of negro slaves. The first edict for this purpose is said to have been one in April, 1615, and another was made in May, 1685, which is not confined to negroes, but regulates the general police in the French islands in America, and is known by the name of the Code Noir. But notwithstanding these edicts, if negro slaves were carried from the French American islands into France, they were entitled to the benefit of the ancient French law, and became free on their arrival in France. To prevent this consequence, a third edict was made in October, 1716, which permits the bringing of negro slaves into France from their American islands. The permission is granted under various restrictions, all tending to prevent the long continuance of negroes in France, to restrain their owners from treating them as property whilst they continue in their mother country, and to prevent the importation of fugitive negroes; and with a like view, a royal declaration was made in December, 1738, containing an exposition of the edict of 1716, and some additional provisions. But the ancient law of France in favour of slaves from another country, still has effect, if the terms of the edict of 1716, and of the declaration of 1738 are not strictly complied with; or if the negro is brought from a place to which they do not extend. This appears from two cases adjudged since the edict of 1716. In one of these, which happened in 1728, a negro had been brought from the island of St. Domingo without observing the terms of the edict of 1716; and in the other, which was decided so late as the year 1758, a slave had been brought from the East Indies, to which the edict doth not extend: and in both these cases the slaves were declared to be free. Such are the examples drawn from the laws and usages of other European countries, and they fully evince, that wherever it is the policy to discountenance slavery, a disregard of the *lex loci*, in the case of slavery, is as well justified by general practice as it is really founded on necessity. Nor is the justice of such proceeding less evident; for how can it be unjust to divest the master's property in his slave when he is carried into a country, in which for the wisest and most humane reasons, such property is known to be prohibited, and consequently cannot be lawfully introduced?

6. It may be contended, that though the law of England will not receive the negro as a slave, yet it may suspend the severe qualities of the slavery whilst the negro is in England, and preserve the master's right over him in the relation of a servant, either by presuming a contract for that purpose, or, without the aid of such a refinement, by compulsion of law, grounded on the condition of slavery in which the negro was previous to his arrival here.

But insuperable difficulties occur against modifying and qualifying the slavery by this artificial refinement. In the present case, at all events, such a modification cannot be allowable; because, in the return, the master claims the benefit of the relation between him and the negro in the full extent of the original slavery. But, for the sake of showing the futility of the argument of modification, and in order to prevent a future attempt by the masters of negroes to avail themselves of it, I will try its force.

As to the presuming a contract of service against the negro, I ask at what time is its commencement to be supposed? If the time was before the negro's arrival in England, it was made when he was in a state of slavery, and consequently without the power of contracting. If the time presumed was subsequent, the presumption must begin the moment of the negro's arrival here, and consequently be founded on the mere fact of that arrival, and the consequential enfranchisement by operation of law. But is not a slavery, determined against the consent of the master, a strange foundation for presuming a contract between him and the slave? For a moment however, I will allow the reasonableness of presuming such a contract, or I will suppose it to be reduced to writing; but then I ask, what are the terms of this contract? To answer the master's purpose, it must be a contract to serve the master here; and when he leaves this country to return with him into America, where the slavery will again attach upon the negro. In plain terms, it is a contract to go into slavery whenever the master's occasions shall require. Will the law of England disallow the introduction of slavery, and therefore emancipate the negro from it; and yet give effect to a contract founded solely upon slavery, in slavery ending? Is it possible, that the law of England can be so insulting to the negro, so inconsistent with itself?

The argument of modification, independently of contract, is equally delusive. There is no known rule by which the court can guide itself in a partial reception of slavery. Besides, if the law of England would receive the slavery of the negro in any way, there can be no reason why it should not be admitted in the same degree as the slavery of the villein; but the argument of modification necessarily supposes the contrary; because, if the slavery of the negro was received in the same extent, then it would not be necessary to have recourse to a qualification. There is also one other reason still more repugnant to the idea of modifying the slavery. If the law of England would modify the slavery, it would certainly take away its most exceptionable qualities, and leave those which are least oppressive. But the modification required will be insufficient for the master's purpose, unless the law leaves behind a quality the most exceptionable, odious, and oppressive; an arbitrary power of reviving the slavery in its full extent, by removal of the negro to a place in which the slavery will again attach upon him with all its original severity.

From this examination of the several objections in favour of slavery in England, I think myself well warranted to observe, that, instead of being weakened, the arguments against slavery in England have derived an additional force. The result is, not merely that negroes become free on being brought into this country, but that the law of England confers the gift of liberty entire and unincumbered; not in name only, but really and substantially; and consequently that Mr. Steuart cannot have the least right over Sommersett the negro, either in the open character of a slave, or in the disguised one of an ordinary servant.

II. In the outset of the argument I made a second question on Mr. Steuart's authority to enforce his right, if he has any, by transporting the negro out of England. Few words will be necessary on this point, which my duty as counsel for the negro requires me to make, in order to give him every possible chance of a discharge from his confinement, and not from any doubt of success on the question of slavery.

If in England the negro continues a slave to Mr. Steuart, he must be content to have the negro subject to those limitations which the laws of villenage imposed on the lord in the enjoyment of his property in the villein; their being no other laws to regulate slavery in this country. But even those laws did not permit that high act of dominion which Mr. Steuart has exercised; for they restrained the lord from forcing the villein out of England. The law, by which the lord's power over his villein was thus limited, has reached the present time. It is a law made in the time of the first William, and the words of it are, *prohibemus ut nullus vendat hominem extra patriam.*

If Mr. Steuart had claimed the negro as a servant by contract, and in his return to the *habeas corpus* had stated a written agree- ment to leave England as Mr. Steuart should require, signed by the negro, and made after his arrival in England, when he had a capacity of contracting, it might then have been a question, whether such a contract in writing would have warranted Mr. Steuart in compelling the performance of it, by forcibly transporting the negro out of his country? I am myself satisfied, that no contract, however solemnly entered into, would have justified such violence. It is contrary to the genius of the English law to allow any enforcement of agree ments or contacts by any other compulsion than that from our courts of justice. The exercise of such a power is not lawful in cases of agreements of property; much less ought it to be so for enforcing agreements against the person. Besides, is it reasonable to suppose, that the law of England would permit that against the servant by contract, which is denied against the slave? Nor are great authorities wanting to acquit the law of England of such an incon- sistency, and to show that a contract will not warrant a compulsion by imprisonment, and consequently much less by transporting the party out of this kingdom. Lord Hobart, whose extraordinary learning, judgment, and abilities, have always ranked his opinion amongst the highest authorities of law, expressly says that "the body of a freeman cannot be made subject to distress or imprison ment by contract, but only by judgment." There is, however, one case, in which it is said that the performance of a service to be done abroad may be compelled without the intervention of a court of justice: I mean the case of an infant apprentice, bound by proper indentures to a mariner or other person, where the nature of the service imports that it is to be done out of the kingdom, and the party, by reason of his infancy, is liable to a coercion not justifiable in ordinary cases. The Habeas Corpus Act goes a step further; and persons who, by contract in writing, agree with a merchant or owner of a plantation, or any other person, to be transported beyond sea, and receive earnest on such agreements, are excepted from the benefit of that statute. I must say, that the exception appears very unguarded; and if the law, as it was previous to this statute, did entitle the subject to the *habeas corpus* in the case which the statute excepts, it can only operate in excluding him in that particular case from the additional provisions of the statute, and cannot, I presume, be justly extended to deprive him of the *habeas corpus* as the common law gave it before the making of the statute.

Upon the whole, the return to the *habeas corpus* in the present case, in whatever way it is considered, whether by inquiry into the foundation of Mr. Steuart's right to the person and service of the negro, or by reference to the violent manner in which it has been attempted to enforce that right, will appear equally unworthy of this court's approbation. By condemning the return, the revival of domestic slavery will be rendered as impracticable by introduction from our colonies and from other countries, as it is by commencement here. Such a judgment will be no less conducive to the public advantage, than it will be conformable to natural justice, and to principles and authorities of law ; and this court, by effectually obstructing the admission of the new slavery of negroes into England, will in these times reflect as much honour on themselves, as the great judges, their predecessors, formerly acquired, by contributing to uniformly and successfully to the suppression of the old slavery of villenage.

ARGUMENTS OF THE OTHER COUNSEL.

Mr. ALLEYNE.—Though it may seem presumption in me to offer any remarks, after the elaborate discourse just now delivered, yet I hope the indulgence of the Court ; and shall confine my observations to some few points, not included by Mr. Hargrave. It is well known to your lordships, that much has been asserted by the ancient philosophers and civilians in defence of the principles of slavery ; Aristotle has particularly enlarged on that subject. An observation still it is, of one of the most able, most ingenious, most convincing writers of modern times, whom I need not hesitate, on this occasion, to prefer to Aristotle, the great Montesquieu, that

Aristotle, on this subject, reasoned very unlike the philosopher. He draws his precedents from barbarous ages and nations, and then deduces maxims from them, for the contemplation and practice of civilized times and countries. If a man who in battle has had his enemy's throat at his sword's point, spares him, and says therefore he has power over his life and liberty, is this true? By whatever duty he was bound to spare him in battle (which he always is when he can with safety), by the same he obliges himself to spare the life of the captive, and restore his liberty as soon as possible, consistent with those considerations from whence he was authorised to spare at first; the same indispensible duty operates throughout. As a contract; in all contracts there must be power on one side to give, on the other to receive; and a competent consideration. Now, what power can there be in any man to dispose of all the rights vested by nature and society in him and his descendants? He cannot consent to part with them, without ceasing to be a man; for they immediately flow from, and are essential to, his condition as such: they cannot be taken from him, for they are not his, as a citizen or a member of society merely; and are not to be resigned to a power inferior to that which gave them. With respect to a consideration, what shall be adequate? As a speculative point, slavery may a little differ in its appearance, and the relation of master and slave, with the obligations on the part of the slave, may be conceived; and merely in this view, might be thought to take effect in all places alike; as natural relations always do. But slavery is not a natural, it is a municipal relation; an institution therefore confined to certain places, and necessarily dropt by passage into a country where such municipal regulations do not subsist. The negro making choice of his habitation here, has subjected himself to the penalties, and is therefore entitled to the protection of our laws. One remarkable case seems to require being mentioned; some Spanish criminals having escaped from execution, were set free in France. [Lord MANSFIELD.—Note the distinction in the case: in this case France was not bound to judge by the municipal laws of Spain; nor was to take cognizance of the offences supposed against that law.] There has been started an objection, that a company having been established by our government for the trade of slaves, it were unjust to deprive them here. No; the government incorporated them with such powers as individuals had used by custom, the only title on which that trade subsisted: I conceive, that had never extended, nor could extend, to slaves brought hither. It was not enlarged at all by the incorporation of that company, as

to the nature or limits of its authority. It is said, let slaves know
hey are all free as soon as arrived here, they will flock over in vast
numbers, over-run this country, and desolate the plantations. There
are too strong penalties by which they will be well kept in; nor are
the persons who might convey them over much induced to attempt
it; the despicable condition in which negroes have the misfortune to
be considered, effectually prevents their importation in any considerable degree. Ought we not on our part to guard and preserve that
liberty by which we are distinguished by all the earth! To be
jealous of whatever measure has a tendency to diminish the venera-
tion due to the first of blessings? The horrid cruelties, scarce
credible in recital, perpetrated in America, might, by the allowance
of slaves amongst us, be introduced here. Could your lordship,
could any liberal and ingenious temper, endure, in the fields border-
ing on this city, to see a wretch bound for some trivial offence to a
tree, torn and agonizing beneath the scourge? Such objects might
by time become familiar, become unheeded by this nation; exercised
as they are now to far different sentiments. May those sentiments
never be extinct! The feelings of humanity! The generous sallies
of free minds! May such principles never be corrupted by the
mixture of slavish customs! Nor can I believe we shall suffer any
individual living here to want that liberty, whose effects are glory
and happiness to the public and every individual.

Mr. WALLACE—The question has been stated, whether the
right can be supported here, or, if it can, whether a course of proceedings at law be not necessary to give effect to the right? It is
found in three quarters of the globe, and in part of the fourth. In
Asia the whole people, in Africa and America far the greater part, in
Europe great numbers of the Russians and Polanders. As to captivity in war, the Christian princes have been used to give life to the
prisoners, and it took rise probably in the Crusades, when they gave
them life, and sometimes enfranchised them, to enlist under the
standard of the cross against the Mahometans. The right of a
conqueror was absolute in Europe, and is in Africa. The natives are
brought from Africa to the West Indies. Purchase is made there,
not because of positive law, but there being no law against it. It
cannot be in consideration by this or any other court, to see whether
the West Indian regulations are the best possible; such as they are,
while they continue in force as laws, they must be adhered to. As
to England not permitting slavery, there is no law against it, nor do
I find any attempt has been made to prove the existence of one.
Villenage itself has all but the name. Though the dissolution of

monasteries, amongst other material alterations, did occasion the
decay of that tenure, slaves could breathe in England; for villeins
were in this country and were mere slaves in Elizabeth. Sheppard's
Abridgment, afterwards, says they were worn out in his time.
[Lord Mansfield mentions an assertion, but does not recollect the
author, that two only were in England in the time of Charles II, at
the time of the abolition of tenures.] In the cases cited, the two
first directly affirm an action of trover, an action appropriated to
mere common chattels. Lord Holt's opinion, is a mere *dictum*, a
decision unsupported by precedent. And if it be objected, that a
proper action could not be brought, it is a known and allowed
practice in mercantile transactions, if the cause arises abroad, to lay
it within the kingdom: therefore the contract in Virginia might be
laid to be in London, and would not be traversable. With respect
to the other cases, the particular mode of action was alone objected
to; had it been an action ' per quod servitium amisit.' for loss of
service, the Court would have allowed it. The Court called the
person, for the recovery of whom it was brought, a slavish servant, in
Chamberlayne's case. Lord Hardwicke, and the afterwards lord
chief justice Talbot, then attorney and solicitor-general, pronounced
a slave not free by coming into England. It is necessary the
masters should bring them over; for they cannot trust the whites,
either with the stores or the navigating the vessel. Therefore the
benefit taken on the Habeas Corpus Act ought to be allowed.

Lord MANSFIELD observes. The case alluded to was upon a
petition in Lincoln's Inn Hall, after dinner; probably, therefore,
might not, as he believes the contrary is not unusual at that hour,
be taken with much accuracy. The principal matter was then, on
the earnest solicitation of many merchants, to know, whether a slave
was freed by being made a Christian? And it was resolved, not.
It is remarkable, though the English took infinite pains before to
prevent their slaves being made Christians, that they might not be
freed, the French suggested they must bring their's into France
(when the edict of 1706 was petitioned for) to make them Christians.
He said the distinction was difficult as to slavery, which could not
be resumed after emancipation, and yet the condition of slavery, in
its full extent, could not be tolerated here. Much consideration
was necessary to define how far the point should be carried.

The Court must consider the great detriment to proprietors, there
being so great a number in the ports of this kingdom, that many
thousands of pounds would be lost to the owners by setting them
free. (A gentleman observed, no great danger, for in a whole fleet,

usually, there would not be six slaves.) As to France, the case stated decides no further than that kingdom : and there freedom was claimed, because the slave had not been registered in the port where he entered, conformably to the edict of 1706. Might not a slave as well be freed by going out of Virginia to the adjacent country, where there are no slaves, if change to a place of contrary custom was sufficient ? A statute by the legislature, to subject the West India property to payment of debts, I hope, will be thought some proof; another act divests the African company of their slaves and vests them in the West India Company : I say, I hope these are proofs the law has interfered for the maintenance of the trade in slaves, and the transferring of slavery. As for want of application, properly to a court of justice, a common servant may be corrected here by his master's private authority. Habeas Corpus acknowledges a right to seize persons by force employed to serve abroad. A right of compulsion there must be, or the master will be under the ridiculous necessity of neglecting his proper business, by staying here to have their service, or must be quite deprived of those he has been obliged to bring over. The case, as to service for life, was not allowed, merely for want of a deed to pass it.

The Court approved Mr. Alleyne's opinion of the distinction. how far municipal laws were to be regarded ; instanced the right of marriage ; which properly solemnized, was in places the same, but the regulations of power over children from it, and other circumstances, very various; and advised, if the merchants thought it so necessary, to apply to parliament, who could make laws.

Adjourned till that day se'nnight.

Mr. DUNNING—It is incumbent on me to justify Captain Knowles's detainer of the negro; this will be effected, by proving a right in Mr. Steuart ; even a supposed one ; for till that matter was determined, it were somewhat unaccountable that a negro should depart his service, and put the means out of his power of trying that right to effect, by a flight out of the kingdom. I will explain what appears to me the foundation of Mr. Steuart's claim. Before the writ of Habeas Corpus issued in the present case, there was, and there still is, a great number of slaves in Africa (from whence the American plantations are supplied), who are saleable, and in fact sold. Under all these descriptions is James Sommersett. Mr. Steuart brought him over to England, purposing to return to Jamaica, the negro chose to depart the service, and was stopt and detained by Captain Knowles, until his master should set sail and take him away to be sold in Jamaica. The gentlemen on the other

side to whom I impute no blame, but on the other hand much commendation, have advanced many ingenious propositions, part of
which are undeniably true, and part (as is usual in compositions of
ingenuity) very disputable. It is my misfortune to address an
audience, the greater part of which, I fear, are prejudiced the other
way. But wishes, I am well convinced, will never enter into your
lordships' minds, to influence the determination of the point : this
cause must be what in fact and law it is. Its fate, I trust, therefore
depends on fixt invariable rules, resulting by law from the nature of
the case. For myself, I would not be understood to intimate a wish
in favour of slavery, by any means, nor on the other side to be supposed the maintainer of an opinion contrary to my own judgment. I
am bound by duty to maintain those arguments which are most
useful to Captain Knowles, as far as is consistent with truth, and if
his conduct has been agreeable to the laws throughout, I am under
a farther indispensable duty to support it. I ask no other attention
than may naturally result from the importance of the question : less
than this I have no reason to expect, more, I neither demand nor
wish to have allowed. Many alarming apprehensions have been
entertained of the consequence of the decision, either way. About
14,000 slaves, from the most exact intelligence I am able to procure,
are at present here, and some little time past, 166,914 in Jamaica.
There are, besides, a number of wild negroes in the woods. The
computed value of a negro in those parts £50 a head. In the other
islands I cannot state with the same accuracy, but on the whole they
are about as many. The means of conveyance, I am told, are
manifold. Every family almost brings over a great number, and
will, be the decision on which side it may. Most negroes who have
money (and that description I believe will include nearly all) make
interest with the common sailors to be carried hither. There are
negroes not falling under the proper denomination of any yet mentioned, descendants of the original slaves, the aborigines, if I may
call them so. These have gradually acquired a natural attachment
to their country and situation. In all insurrections they side with
their masters, otherwise the vast disproportion of the negroes to the
whites (not less probably than that of 100 to 1), would have been
fatal in its consequences. There are very strong and particular
grounds of apprehension, if the relation in which they stand to their
masters is utterly to be dissolved on the instant of their coming into
England. Slavery, say the gentlemen, is an odious thing : the name
is, and the reality, if it were as one has defined, and the rest supposed it. If it were necessary to the idea and the existence of

James Sommersett, that his master, even here, might kill, nay, might
eat him, might sell living or dead, might make him and his descendants property alienable, and thus transmissible to posterity: this
how high soever my ideas may be of the duty of my profession, is
what I should decline pretty much to defend or assert, for any purpose seriously.   I should only speak of it to testify my contempt and
abhorrence.   But this is what at present I am not at all concerned
in, unless Captain Knowles, or Mr. Steuart, have killed or eat him.
Freedom has been asserted as a natural right, and therefore unalienable and unrestrainable.   There is perhaps no branch of this right,
but in some at all times, and in all places at different times, has been
restrained, nor could society otherwise be concieved to exist.   For
the great benefit of the public and individuals, natural liberty, which
consists in doing what one likes, is altered to the doing what one
ought.   The gentlemen who have spoken with so much zeal, have
supposed different ways by which slavery commences, but have
omitted one, and rightly, for it would have given a more favourable
idea of the nature of that power against which they combat.   We are
apt (and great authorities support this way of speaking) to call
those nations universally, whose internal policy we are ignorant of,
barbarians; (thus the Greeks, particularly, stiled many nations,
whose customs, generally considered, were far more justifiable and
commendable than their own :) unfortunately, from calling them barbarians, we are apt to think them so, and draw conclusions accordingly.   There are slaves in Africa by captivity in war, but the
number far from great.   The country is divided into many small,
some great territories, who do, in their wars with one another, use
this custom.   There are of these people, men who have a sense of
the right and value of freedom, but who imagine that offences against
society are punishable justly by the severe law of servitude.   For crimes
against property, a considerable addition is made to the number of
slaves.   They have a process by which the quantity of the debt is
ascertained, and if all the property of the debtor in goods and chattels
is insufficient, he who has thus dissipated all he has besides, is deemed
property himself.   The proper officer (sheriff we may call him) seizes
the insolvent, and disposes of him as a slave.   We don't contend
under which of these the unfortunate man in question is, but his
condition was that of servitude in Africa.   The law of the land of
that country disposed of him as property, with all the consequences
of transmission and alienation.   The statutes of the British legislature confirm this condition, and thus he was a slave both in law and
fact.   I do not aim at proving these points, not because they want

evidence, but because they have not been controverted, to my recollection, and are, I think, incapable of denial. Mr. Steuart, with
this right, crossed the Atlantic, and was not to have the satisfaction
of discovering, till after his arrival in this country, that all relations
between him and the negro, as master and servant, was to be matter
of controversy, and of long legal disquisition. A few words may
be proper, concerning the Russian slave, and the proceedings of the
House of Commons on that case. It is not absurd in the idea, as
quoted, nor improbable as matter of fact. The expression has a kind
of absurdity. I think, without any prejudice to Mr. Steuart, or the
merits of this cause, I may admit the utmost possible to be desired, as
far as the case of that slave goes. The master and slave were both
(or should have been at least), on their coming here, new creatures.
Russian slavery, and even the subordination among themselves, in
the degree they use it, is not here to be tolerated. Mr. Alleyne
justly observes, the municipal regulations of one country are not
binding on another, but does the relation cease where the modes of
creating it, the degress in which it subsists, vary? I have not heard,
nor, I fancy, is there any intention to affirm, the relation of master
and servant ceases here? I understand the municipal relations
differ in different colonies, according to humanity and otherwise. A
distinction was endeavoured to be established between natural and
municipal relations; but the natural relations are not those only
which attend the person of the man, political do so too; with
which the municipal are most closely connected: municipal laws,
strictly, are those confined to a particular place; political, are those
in which the municipal laws of many states may and do concur. The
relation of husband and wife, I think myself warranted in questioning
as a natural relation. Does it subsist for life; or to answer the
natural purposes which may reasonably be supposed often to termi-
nate sooner? Yet this is one of those relations which follow a man
everywhere. If only natural relations had that property, the effect
would be very limited indeed. In fact, the municipal laws are principally employed in determining the manner by which relations are
created, and which manner varies in various countries, and in the
same country at different periods, the political relation itself continuing usually unchanged by the change of place. There is but one
form at present with us, by which the relation of husband and wife
can be constituted; there was a time when otherwise. I need not
say other nations have their own modes, for that and other ends of
society. Contract is not the only means, on the other hand, of producing the relation of master and servant; the magistrates are

empowered to oblige persons under certain circumstances to serve. Let me take notice, neither the air of England is too pure for a slave to breath in, nor have the laws of England rejected servitude Villenage in this country is said to be worn out; the propriety of the expression strikes me a little. Are the laws not existing by which it was created? A matter of more curiosity than use, it is to enquire when that set of people ceased.

The statute of tenures did not however abolish villenage in gross; it left persons of that condition in the same state as before; if their descendants are all dead, the gentlemen are right to say the subject of those laws is gone, but not the law: if the subject revives, the law will lead the subject. If the statute of Charles 2d. ever be repealed, the law of villenage revives in its full force. If my learned brother the serjeant, or the other gentlemen who argued on the supposed subject of freedom, will go through an operation my reading assures me will be sufficient for that purpose, I shall claim them as property. I won't, I assure them, make a rigorous use of my power, I will neither sell them, eat them, nor part with them. It would be a great surprize, and some inconvenience, if a foreigner bringing over a servant, as soon as he got hither, must take care of his carriage, his horse, and himself, in whatever method he might have the luck to invent. He must find his way to London on foot. He tells his servant, Do this: the servant replies, Before I do it, I think fit to inform you, Sir, the first step on this happy land sets all men on a perfect level: yon are just as much obliged to obey my commands. Thus, neither superior, nor inferior, both go without their dinner. We should find singular comfort on entering the limits of a foreign couutry, to be thus at once divested of all attendance and all accommodation. The gentlemen have collected more reading than I have leisure to collect, or industy (I must own) if I had leisure: very laudable pains have been taken, and very ingenious, in collecting the sentiments of other countries, which I shall not much regard, as affecting the point or jurisdiction of this court. In Holland, so far from perfect freedom, (I speak from knowledge) there are, who without being conscious of contract, have for offences perpetual labour imposed, and death the condition annexed to non-performance. Either all the different ranks must be allowed natural, which is not readily conceived, or there are political ones, which cease not on change of soil. But in what manner is the negro to be treated? How far lawful to detain him? My footman according to my agreement, is obliged to attend me from this city, or he is not; if no condition, that he shall not be obliged, from hence he is obliged, and no injury done.

A servant of a sheriff, by the command of his master, laid hand gently on another servant of his master, and brought him before his master, who himself compelled the servant to his duty. An action of assault and battery, and false imprisonment, was brought, and the principal question was, on demurrer, whether the master could command the servant, though he might have justified his taking of the servant by his own hands? The convenience of the public is far better provided for, by this private authority of the master, than if the lawfulness of the command were liable to be litigated every time a servant thought fit to be negligent or troublesome.

Is there a doubt, but a negro might interpose in the defence of a master, or a master in defence of a negro? If to all purposes of advantage, mutuality requires the rule to extend to those of disadvantage. It is said, as not formed by contract, no restraint can be placed by contract. Whichever way it was formed, the consequences, good or ill, follow from the relation, not the manner of producing it. I may observe, there is an establishment by which magistrates compel idle or dissolute persons, of various ranks and denominations, to serve. In the case of apprentices bound out by the parish, neither the trade is left to the choice of those who are to serve, nor the consent of parties necessary ; no contract, therefore, is made in the former instance, none in the latter, the duty remains the same. The case of contract for life, quoted from the year books, was recognized as valid, the solemnity only of an instrument judged requisite. Your lordships (this variety of service, with divers other sorts, existing by law here), have the option of classing him amongst those servants which he most resembles in condition. Therefore, it seems to me, are by law authorised to enforce a service for life in the slave, that being a part of his situation before his coming hither; which, as not incompatible, but agreeing with our laws, may justly subsist here ; I think, I might say, must necessarily subsist, as a consequence of a previous right in Mr. Steuart, which our institutions not dissolving, confirm. I don't insist on all the consequences of villenage ; enough is established for our cause, by supporting the continuance of the service. Much has been endeavoured to raise a distinction, as to the lawfulness of the negroe's commencing slave, from the difficulty or impossibility of discovery by what means, under what authority, he became such. This, I apprehend, if a curious search were made, not utterly inexplicable; nor the legality of his original servitude difficult to be proved. But to what end? Our legislature, where it finds a relation existing, supports it in all

suitable consequences, without using to enquire how it commenced.
A man enlists for no specified time. The contract in construction of
law, is for a year. The legislature, when once the man is enlisted,
interposes annually to continue him in the service, as long as the
public has need of him. In times of public danger, he is forced into
the service; the laws from thence forward find him a soldier, make
him liable to all the burden, confer all the rights (if any rights there
are of that state), and enforce all penalties of neglect of any duty in
that profession, as much and as absolutely, as if by contract he had
so disposed of himself. If the Court see a necessity of entering into
the large field of argument, as to the right of the unfortunate man,
and service appears to them deducible from a discussion of that
nature to him, I neither doubt they will, nor wish they should not.
As to the purpose of Mr. Steuart and Captain Knowles, my argument does not require trover should lie, as for recovering of property,
nor trespass. A form of action there is, the writ Per Quod Servitum
Amisit, for loss of service, which the Court would have recognized.
If they allowed the means of suing a right, they allowed the right.
The opinion cited to prove the negroes free on coming hither, only
declares them not saleable, does not take away their service. I would
say, before I conclude, not for the sake of the Court, of the audience.
The matter now in question, interests the zeal for freedom of no
person, if truly considered, it being only, whether I must apply to a
court of justice (in a case, where if the servant was an Englishman I
might use my private authority to enforce the performance of the
service according to its nature), or may, without force or outrage,
take my servant myself or by another. I hope, therefore, I shall not
suffer in the opinion of those whose honest passions are fired at the
name of slavery. I hope I have not transgressed my duty to
humanity, nor doubt I your lordship's discharge of yours to justice.

DAVY, Serj.—My learned friend has thought proper to consider
the question in the beginning of his speech, as of great importance :
it is indeed so; but not for those reasons principally assigned by him.
I apprehend, my lord, the honour of England, the honour of the laws
of every Englishman, here or abroad, is now concerned. He observes,
the number is 14,000 or 15,000; if so, high time to put an end to
the practice; more especially since they must be sent back as slaves,
though servants here. The increase of such inhabitants, not
interested in the prosperity of a country, is very pernicious; in an
island, which can, as such, not extend its limits, nor consequently
maintain more than a certain number of inhabitants, dangerous in excess. Money from foreign trade (or any other means)

is not the wealth of a nation, nor conduces anything to support it, any farther than the produce of the earth will answer the demand of necessaries. In that case money enriches the inhabitants, as being the common representative of those necessaries. But this represention is merely imaginary and useless, if the increase of people exceeds the annual stock of provisions requisite for their subsistence. Thus, foreign superfluous inhabitants augmenting perpetually, are ill to be allowed; a nation of enemies in the heart of a state, still worse. Mr. Dunning availed himself of a wrong interpretation of the word 'natural:' it was not used in the sense in which he thought fit to understand that expression: it was used as moral, which no laws can supersede. All contracts, I do not venture to assert, are of a moral nature, but I know not any law to confirm an immoral contract, and execute it. The contract of marriage is a moral contract, established for moral purposes, enforcing moral obligations; the right of taking property by descent, the legitimacy of children; (who in France are considered legitimate, though born before the marriage, in England not): these, and many other consequences, flow from the marriage properly solemnized; are governed by the municipal laws of that particular state, under whose institutions the contracting and disposing parties live as subjects, and by whose established forms they submit the relation to be regulated, so far as its consequences, not concerning the moral obligation, are interested. In the case of Thorn and Watkins, in which your lordship was counsel, determined before Lord Hardwicke—A man died in England, with effects in Scotland; having a brother of the whole and a sister of the half blood: the latter, by the laws of Scotland, could not take. The brother applies for administration to take the whole estate, real and personal, into his own hands, for his own use; the sister files a bill in Chancery. The then Mr. Attorney-General puts in answer for the defendent; and affirms, the estate, as being in Scotland, and descending from a Scotchman, should be governed by that law. Lord Hardwicke overruled the objection against the sister's taking, declared there was no pretence for it, and spoke to this effect, and nearly in the following words—" Suppose a foreigner has effects in our stocks, and dies abroad, they must be distributed according to the laws, not of the place where his effects were, but of that to which as a subject he belonged at his death." All relations governed by municipal laws, must be so far dependant on them, that if the parties change their country the municipal laws give way, if contradictory to the political regulations of that other country, (See the cases cited in Fabrigas

v. Mostyn, *inf.*) In the case of master and slave, being no moral
obligation, but founded on principles, and supported by practice,
utterly foreign to the laws and customs of this country, the law
cannot recognize such relation. The arguments founded on municipal regulations, considered in their proper nature, have been
treated so fully, so learnedly, and ably, as scarce to leave any room
for observations on that subject : any thing I could offer to enforce,
would rather appear to weaken the proposition, compared with the
strength and propriety with which that subject has already been
explained and urged. I am not concerned to dispute, the negro
may contract to serve, nor deny the relation between them, while he
continues under his original proprietor's roof and protection. It is
remarkable, in all Dyer, (for I have caused a search to be made as
far as the 4th of Henry the 8th,) there is not one instance of a
man's being held a villein who denied himself to be one ; nor can I
find a confession of villenage in those times. [Lord Mansfield :—
The last confession of villenage extant, is in the 19th of Henry the
6th.] If the court would acknowledge the relation of master and
servant, it certainly would not allow the most exceptionable part of
slavery : that of being obliged to remove, at the will of the master,
from the protection of this land of liberty, to a country where there
are no laws, or hard laws to insult him. It will not permit slavery
suspended for a while, suspended during the pleasure of the master.
The instance of master and servant commencing without contract ;
and that of apprentices against the will of the parties, (the latter
found in its consequences exceedingly pernicious ;) both these are
provided by special statutes of our own municipal law. If made in
France, or any where but here, they would not have been binding
here. To punish not even a criminal for offences against the laws of
another country ; to set free a galley-slave, who is a slave by his
crime ; and make a slave of a negro, who is one by his complexion ;
is a cruelty and absurdity that I trust will never take place here :
such as, if promulged, would make England a disgrace to all the
nations under heaven : for the reducing a man, guiltless of any
offence against the laws, to the condition of slavery, the worst and
most abject state. Mr. Dunning has mentioned, what he is pleased
to term philosophical and moral grounds, I think, or something to
that effect, of slavery ; and would not by any means have us think
disrespectfully of those nations, whom we mistakenly call barbarians,
merely for carrying on that trade : for my part, we may be warranted, I believe, in affirming the morality or propriety of the
practice does not enter their heads ; they make slaves of whom they

think fit. For the air of England; I think, however, it has been gradually purifying ever since the reign of Elizabeth. Mr. Dunning seems to have discovered so much, as he finds it changes a slave into a servant; though unhappily he does not think it of efficacy enough to prevent that pestilent disease reviving, the instant the poor man is obliged to quit (voluntarily quits, and legally it seems we ought to say,) this happy country. However, it has been asserted, and is now repeated by me, this air is too pure for a slave to breathe in: I trust I shall not quit this court without certain conviction of the truth of that ascertion.

Lord MANSFIELD.—The question is, if the owner had a right to detain the slave, for the sending of him over to be sold in Jamaica. In five or six cases of this nature, I have known it to be accommodated by agreement between the parties: on its first coming before me, I strongly recommended it here. But if the parties will have it decided, we must give our opinion. Compassion will not, on the one hand, nor inconvenience on the other, be to decide; but the law: in which the difficulty will be principally from the inconvenience on both sides. Contract for sale of a slave is good here; the sale is a matter to which the law properly and readily attaches, and will maintain the price according to the agreement. But here the person of the slave himself is immediately the object of enquiry; which makes a very material difference. The now question is, Whether any dominion, authority or coercion can be exercised in this country, on a slave according to the American laws? The difficulty of adopting the relation, without adopting it in all its consequences, is indeed extreme; and yet, many of those consequences are absolutely contrary to the municipal law of England. We have no authority to regulate the conditions in which law shall operate. On the other hand should we think the coercive power cannot be exercised: it is now about 50 years since the opinion given by two of the greatest men of their own or any times, (since which no contract has been brought to trial, between the masters and slaves;) the service performed by the slaves without wages is a clear indication they did not think themselves free by coming hither. The setting 14,000 or 15,000 men at once loose by a solemn opinion, is very disagreeable in the effects it threatens There is a case in Hobart (Coventry and Woodfall), where a man had contracted to go as a mariner: but the now case will not come within that decision. Mr. Steuart advances no claims on contract; he rests his whole demand on a right to the negro as slave, and mentions the purpose of detainure to be the sending of him over to be sold in Jamaica. If the parties will have judgment, 'fiat justitia, ruat cœlum;' let justice be done whatever be the consequence. 50*l.* a-head may not be a high price; then a loss follows to the proprietors of above 700,000*l.* sterling. How would the law stand with respect to their settlement; their wages? How many actions for any slight coercion by the master? We cannot in any of these points direct the law, the law must rule us. In these particulars, it may be matter of weighty consideration, what provisions are made or set by law. Mr. Steuart may end the question, by discharging or giving freedom to the negro. I did think at first to put the matter to a more solemn way of argument: but if my brothers agree, there seems no occasion. I do not imagine, after the point has been discussed on both sides so extremely well, any new light could be thrown on the subject. If the parties choose to refer it to the Common Pleas, they can give themselves that satisfaction whenever they think fit. An application to parliament, if the merchants think the question of great commercial concern, is the best, and perhaps the only method of settling the point for the future. The Court is greatly obliged to the gentlemen of the bar who have spoke on the subject, and by whose care and abilities so much has been effected, that the rule of decision will be reduced to a very easy compass. I cannot omit to express particular happiness in seeing young men, just called to the bar, have been able so much to profit by their reading. I think it right the matter should stand over; and if we are called on for decision, proper notice shall be given.

TRINITY TERM, JUNE 22, 1772.

Lord MANSFIELD.—On the part of Sommersett, the case which we gave notice should be decided this day, the Court now proceeds to give its opinion. I shall recite the return to the writ of Habeas Corpus, as the ground of our determination, omitting only words of form. The captain of the ship on board of which the negro was taken, makes his return to the writ in terms signifying that there have been, and still are, slaves to a great number in Africa, and that the trade in them is authorized by the laws and opinions of Virginia and Jamaica; that they are goods and chattels, and, as such, saleable and sold. That James Sommersett is a negro of Africa, and long before the return of the king's writ was brought to be sold, and was sold to Charles Steuart, Esq., then in Jamaica, and has not been manumitted since. That Mr. Steuart, having occasion to transact business, came over hither, with an intention to return, and brought Sommersett to attend and abide with him, and to carry him back as soon as the business should be transacted. That such intention has been, and still continues, and that the negro did remain till the time of his departure in the service of his master, Mr. Steuart, and quitted it without his consent, and thereupon, before the return of the king's writ, the said Charles Steuart did commit the slave on board the Ann and Mary, to safe custody, to be kept till he should set sail, and then to be taken with him to Jamaica, and there sold as a slave. And this is the cause why he, Captain Knowles,, who was then and now is, commander of the above vessel, and then and now lying in the river of Thames, did the said negro committed to his custody, detain, and on which he now renders him to the orders of the Court. We pay all due attention to the opinion of Sir Philip Yorke, and Lord Chancellor Talbot, whereby they pledged themselves to the British planters, for all the legal consequences of slaves coming over to this kingdom or being baptized, recognized by Lord Hardwicke, sitting as Chancellor on the 19th October, 1749, that trover would lie: that a notion had prevailed, if a negro came over, or became a Christian, he was emancipated, but no ground in law. That he and Lord Talbot, when attorney and solicitor-general, were of opinion, that no such claim for freedom was valid. That though the statute of tenures had abolished villeins regardant to a manor, yet he did not conceive but that a man might still become a villein in gross, by confessing himself such in open court. We are all so well agreed, that we think there is no occasion of having it argued (as I intimated an intention at first), before all the judges, as is usual, for obvious reasons, on a return to a Habeas Corpus. The only question before is, whether the cause on the return is sufficient? If it is, the negro must be remanded; if it is not, he must be discharged. Accordingly, the return states, that the slave departed and refused to serve; whereupon he was kept, to be sold abroad. So high an act of dominion must be recognized by the law of the country where it is used. The power of a master over his slave has been extremely different, in different countries. The state of slavery is of such a nature, that it is incapable of being introduced on any reasons, moral or political, but only by positive law, which preserves its force long after the reasons, occasion, and time itself from whence it was created, is erased from memory. It is so odious that nothing can be suffered to support it, but positive law. Whatever inconveniences, therefore, may follow from the decision, I cannot say this case is allowed or approved by the law of England; and therefore the black must be discharged.

JOHN FORBES AGAINST SIR ALEXANDER INGLIS COCKRANE, KNIGHT, AND SIR GEORGE COCKBURN, KNIGHT.

Barnewall and Cresswell Reports, vol. ii., p. 448.

Where certain persons who had been slaves in a foreign country where slavery was tolerated by law, escaped thence and got on board a British ship of war on the high seas : Held, that a British subject resident in that country, who claimed the slaves as property, could not maintain an action against the commander of the ship for harbouring the slaves after notice.

THE DECLARATION stated that the plaintiff was lawfully possessed of a certain Cotton Plantation, situate in parts beyond the seas—to wit, in East Florida—of large value ; and on which plantation, he employed divers persons, his slaves or servants. The first Count charged the defendant with enticing the slaves away. The second Count stated, that the slaves or servants having wrongfully and against the plaintiff's will, quitted and left the plantation and the plaintiff's service, and gone into the power, care, and keeping of the defendants ; they, knowing them to be the slaves or servants of the plaintiff, wrongfully received the slaves into their custody, and harboured, detained, and kept them from the plaintiff's service. The last count was for wrongfully harbouring, detaining, and keeping the slaves or servants of the plaintiff after notice given to the defendants that the slaves were the plaintiff's property, and request made to the defendants by the plaintiff, to deliver them up to him : pleas—Not guilty. At the trial, before Abbott C. J., at the London sittings, after Trinity term, 1822, a verdict was found for the plaintiff, damages £3,800, subject to the opinion of the Court on the following case :—

The plaintiff was a British merchant, in the Spanish provinces of East and West Florida, where he had carried on trade for a great many years ; and was principally resident at Pensacola, in West Florida. East and West Florida were part of the dominions of the King of Spain ; and Spain was in amity with Great Britain. The plaintiff, before and at the time of the alleged grievances, was the proprietor and in the possession of a Cotton Plantation, called San Pablo, lying contiguous to the river St. John's, in the province of East Florida, and of about 100 negro slaves, whom he had purchased, and who were employed by him upon his plantation. The river St. John's is about thirty or forty miles from the confines of Georgia, one of the United States of America, which is separated from East Florida by the river St. Mary ; and Cumberland Island is at the mouth of the river St. Mary, on the side next Georgia and forms part of that state. During the late war between Great Britain and America, in the month of February, 1815, the defendant, Vice-Admiral Sir Alexander Inglis Cochrane was Commander-in-chief of his Majesty's ships and vessels on the North American station. The other defendant, Rear-admiral Sir George Cockburn, was the second in command upon the said station, and his flag-ship was the Albion. The British forces had taken possession of Cumberland Island; and at that time, occupied and garrisoned the same. The Albion, Terror Bomb, and others of his Majesty's ships of war, formed a squadron under Sir George Cockburn's immediate command off that Island, where the head-quarters of the expedition were. Sir Alexander Cochrane was not off Georgia during the war; and at the time of the capture of the Island, he was at a very considerable distance to the southward of Cumberland Island; but Sir George Cockburn was in correspondence with him while he was at the said Island. In the year 1814, a proclamation had been published by the said Sir Alexander Cochrane, as such Commander-in-chief, and Sir George Cockburn had received great numbers of copies thereof, whilst the ships under his command were lying off the Chesapeake, and distributed them at the Chesapeake, and amongst the different ships; but none were distributed by the order of the defendant, Sir G. Cockburn, to the southward of the Chesapeake—the southern extremity of which, is full 400 miles distant from Cumberland Island. The proclamation stated that it had been represented to him, Sir A. Cochrane, "That many persons then resident in the United States, had expressed a desire to withdraw therefrom, with a view of entering into his Majesty's service, or of being received as free settlers into some of his Majesty's colonies; and it then notified, "that all those who might be disposed to emigrate from the United States would, with their families, be received on board his Majesty's ships or vessels of war, or, at the military posts that might be established upon or near the Coasts of the United States, when they would have their choice of either entering into his Majesty's sea or land forces, or of being sent as free settlers to the British possessions in North America or the West Indies, where they would meet with all due encouragement." One of these proclamations was seen on Amelia Island, East Florida, which is less than a mile from Cumberland Island, and about thirty miles from San Pablo plantation. In the night of the 23rd February, 1815, a number of the plaintiff's slaves deserted from his said plantation, and on the following day, thirty-eight of them were found on board the Terror Bomb, part of the

squadron at Cumberland Island, and entered on her Muster-books as
refugees from Saint John's. It was reported that they came from
seaward; they were mixed with other refugees, and they all spoke
English. On the 26th of the same month of February, Sir George
Cockburn received from the plaintiff a memorial—stating t at the
plaintiff had been a resident in the Spanish provinces of East and
West Florida for nearly thirty years, as clerk and partner of a
mercantile house, established under the particular sanction of the
Spanish Government, for the purpose of trade with the southern
nations of Indians; and which they were allowed to continue by
special permission from his Britannic Majesty, pending the two
Spanish wars that occurred during that period. The said mercantile
house had acquired considerable property in these provinces; and
particularly that the plaintiff possessed in East Florida, a cotton
plantation on the river Saint John's, of which he was sole proprietor,
and held the same with upwards of 100 negroes at the period of the
invasion of the State Georgia, by his Britannic Majesty's forces under
the command of him, Sir G. Cockburn, in January preceding;
that, on the night of the 23rd instant, sixty-two of his
said negroes deserted from the plaintiff's plantation, (together
with four others belonging to Lindsay Tod his manager), of whom
he had found thirty-four, namely, eighteen men, eight women, and
twelve young children of both sexes, together with the aforesaid
four negroes belonging to Mr. Tod, on board of his Majesty's ship
"Terror," Captain Sheridan. But that the said slaves refused to
return to their duty, under pretence that they were then free, in
consequence of having come to this island in possession of his
Britannic Majesty. The plaintiff therefore prayed. "that the
defendant, Sir G. Cockburn, would order the said thirty-eight slaves
to be forthwith delivered to him, their lawful proprietor, together
with the boat which they had piratically stolen from his plantation."
To this memorial a written answer was sent. A correspondence also
took place between the Spanish governor of East Florida and Sir G.
Cockburn, relative to the desertion of the slaves from the Spanish
settlements. This correspondence was previous to Mr. Forbes'
letter or memorial, and after the memorial the plaintiff had an inter-
view with the defendant, Sir G. Cockburn, and claimed of him the
slaves in question, then on board the "Terror," as his property.
Sir G. Cockburn told him he might see his slaves, and use any arguments and persuasion he chose to induce them to return. The
plaintiff accordingly endeavoured to persuade them to go back to
his plantation, and no restraint was put upon them, but they refused

to go. The plaintiff then urged his claim very strongly to Sir G. Cockburn, and said he must get redress if he did not succeed in prevailing upon Sir G. Cockburn to order them back again, which Sir G. Cockburn said he could not do, because they were free agents and might do as they pleased and that he could not force them back. They were victualled and subsisted with Sir G. Cockburn's knowledge whilst on board the Terror Bomb, and on the 6th March were removed from that ship by Sir G. Cockburn's orders into his ship, " The Albion." On the 9th March, 1815, Sir Alexander Inglis Cochrane addressed to Sir G. Cockburn the following letter :

"Sir,—Having received and considered your letter, No. 25, of the 28th February, 1815, and the correspondence it encloses respecting some individuals of colour, who have arrived at Cumberland island, and there placed themselves under the protection of his majesty, and who have been since represented as having escaped from his Catholic majesty's possession in East Florida, where it is said they were slaves, and in consequence have been formally demanded by the governor and other claimants of East Florida, I have the honour to inform you, that under the circumstances attending these people, I do not consider myself authorised (without reference to his Majesty's government) to decide upon the claims set forth by the governor and other persons in East Florida, and, as without such reference, it will be impossible for me to attend to any solicitation of their being given up, you will be pleased to cause the refugees in question to be put on board one of his Majesty's ships going to Bermuda, to be reported to me on their arrival there, and I will take care to have them so guarded as to prevent their desertion and to be forthcoming, should it be decided that they are to be returned to East Florida."

In the same month of March, Sir G. Cockburn sailed in the Albion with the said slaves on board for Bermuda, at which time he had received intelligence of peace between this country and America, and such slaves as belonged to American subjects, and were in the possession of the defendants, were not taken away in consequence of the wording of the treaty of peace. Bermuda is a British colony, 500 miles from East Florida, or any other land where slavery is acknowledged. The slaves in question were, on the 29th March, 1815, transferred by Sir G. Cockburn's orders, from his Majesty's ship Albion into his Majesty's ship Ruby, at Bermuda, and after being on board that ship about twelve months, were landed in that island, and many of them employed in the king's dock-yard there. The slaves which were taken on board the

Albion, and belonging to the plaintiff, were worth to him £3,800

COMYN for the plaintiff. The plaintiff had a property in his slaves, and having been deprived of that property by the act of the defendant, is entitled to maintain this action. Although, by the 47 G. 3, c. 36, the traffic in slaves has been declared unlawful in a British subject, the courts of this country still have respect to the trade itself when carried on by the subjects of a State which continues to tolerate it. Fortuna (a) Donna Marianna (b). The trade is now considered primâ facie illegal, and the burden of proof that it is not so, is thrown upon those who carry it on Amedie (c). If this be the law with respect to a trade which one branch of the Legislature of this country (as appears by the preamble of the Stat. 51, G. 3, c. 23) has pronounced to the contrary to the principles of justice and humanity, a fortiori it must prevail with respect to the rights of property in slaves in the subjects of a foreign country, especially when it is considered that slavery is recognised by the legislature in our own West India islands. It is true that in this country slavery does not exist, but an action is maintainable for the price of slaves in the courts of this country. In Butts v. Penny (d) trover was brought for ten negroes. Upon special verdict it appeared by an examination of the record, that the action was brought to recover the value of negroes, of which the plaintiff had been possessed in India. It is stated in the report that the court held that negroes being usually bought and sold among merchants in India, and being Infidels, there might be a property in them sufficient to maintain the action. It appears that no judgment was ever pronounced. The opinion of the Court, however, is an authority to show that the right of property in slaves, in a country where slavery is allowed, will be recognised by the laws of this country. In Smith v. Gould, (e) the action was brought for a negro wrongfully detained in a country where slavery was lawful. This distinction also was acted upon by the Court in Smith v. Brown (f) and Cooper, and it is recognized in Sommersett's case.(g) These authorities fully establish that this plaintiff had a property in these slaves while in Florida. They made their escape and got on board a British ship, of which one of the defendants, Sir G. Cockburn was the commander. He had notice that they were the property of the plaintiff, and Blake v. Lanyson (h) is an authority to show that an

---

action will lie for harbouring an apprentice, after notice that he is the apprentice of the plaintiff, and by parity of reasoning, the present action is maintainable. The other defendant, Sir A. Cochrane, having concurred in the harbouring of these men, is also liable to be sued.

JERVIS, contra. It may be conceded, that by the laws of a particular country, one man may have a property in others as slaves, and that an action may be maintained by him in the courts of this country, for an injury done to that property, while such his property in the slaves *continued.* Here, all rights of the plaintiff over those persons (who in Florida had been his slaves) ceased the *moment* when they got on board the British ship of war. In Sommersett's case, it was decided, that a person who had been a slave in one of our own settlements, and came to this country, and was here detained by a captain of a ship for the purpose of taking him back to such settlement, was entitled to be set at liberty, inasmuch as the law of England did not recognise the state of slavery. Lord Mansfield says, "The state of slavery is of such a nature, that it is incapable of being introduced on any reasons, moral or political but only by positive law." It is incumbent on the plaintiff in this case; therefore, to shew, that at the time when he demanded these slaves to be given up to him, they were *his* slaves by the positive law of the place where they *then* were. Now it is clear, that the law of England prevailed on board the British ship. Madrazzo *v.* Willes (*a*) is an authority upon that point; for in that case, the Spanish law was recognised by our courts as prevailing on board the Spanish ship, and the slaves were, therefore, considered as property. By parity of reason, these persons who had been slaves, ceased to be slaves the moment that they came on board the British ship; because, by the law of England, slavery is not allowed to exist. Smith *v.* Brown and Cooper, (*b*) too, is an authority to shew, that, in order to maintain an action for the price of a slave, it must be shewn on the face of the pleadings—that the parties were slaves by the law of the particular place where the sale took place. The right to property in slaves, therefore, is conferred by the municipal law of the place only, and can be enforced only for an injury to such property, while the slave is within that place. If a British subject, resident in such a country, committed a violation of such a right, he might possibly be answerable for it in the courts of this country. The right, however, being created only by the municipal law, must be co-extensive with it. If a master, therefore,

---

(*a*) B & A 353. (*b*) 2 Salk., 666.

brings his slave to a place where slavery is unlawful, an action is not
maintainable against another person for detaining or harbouring the
slave, because there is no obligation on the latter to return to the
service from which he has escaped.

BAYLEY, J. It is a matter of great satisfaction to me that this
case, which is one of considerable importance, and of some novelty,
may, at the option of either party, be turned into a special verdict.
At present the impression upon my mind is, that the action is not
maintainable. The cases decided in the Admiralty Courts, are not
applicable to the present. There certain persons had taken upon
themselves to be active, and to seize ships having slaves on board, on
the ground that they had a right so to do, either by the law of
nations or the law of this country. The Court of Admiralty refused
to assist the captors in condemning that property, to which the
claimants, by the law of the particular country to which they
belonged, had a right. In such cases, the Court of Admiralty is
called upon to act between the two countries upon a common
principle applicable to both. That court, therefore, cannot lend its
assistance in the condemnation of a vessel, on the ground that it is
engaged in a traffic which, according to the municipal laws of the
country to which the claimant belongs, is no wrong. The captain of
Fortuna had done no act that subjected him to condemnation by the
laws of his own country, and this country had no right to say that
he had been doing wrong, or that his property was subject to condemnation. In substance, therefore, the decision of that court
operates only in the nature of an *amoveas manus*, and no more.
In Madrazzo *v.* Willes, the defendant had taken upon himself
to be active, and to seize the ship and slaves, and the
court held that he had no right to make the seizure. Having
thus disposed of the authorities referred to in argument, I now
come to consider the question for our decision. My opinion in
this case does not at all proceed upon the ground that slavery is not to
be tolerated in the place where the slaves came on board, nor that
an action, under circumstances, may not be maintained for enticing
away or harbouring a slave, nor on the ground that the instant he
leaves his master's plantation and gets upon other land, where slavery
is not tolerated, that *ex necessitate*, he becomes, to all intents and
purposes, a free man. I give no opinion upon any one of these
points, but I say that there is a great distinction between making
the law of England active, and leaving the law of England passive.
In the cases cited from the Admiralty Courts, the law of England
was passive. Here we are called upon to put that law into activity

upon the ground that the defendants have done a wrong. I am of opinion, however, that we are not warranted in coming to that conclusion, with reference to the character which the defendants at that time were filling. The ground of complaint alleged in the first count of the declaration is, that the defendant enticed the slaves : there is no evidence to support that count. The second count charges that the defendants harboured the slaves, knowing them to be the slaves of the plaintiff : and the third count, that they harboured them after notice. Blake v. Lanyon (a) is an authority to show that the latter is a good ground of action. It is unnecessary, therefore, to consider whether there was evidence to shew that the defendants knew the slaves to belong to the plaintiff. But a very material allegation in all the counts is, that the defendants wrongfully did the act with which they were charged: the question is, whether that allegation was made out against either of the defendants. In Blake v. Lanyon the defendant must have had full opportunity of making enquiry, and satisfying himself, whether that which was asserted on the part of the plaintiff was true or not, there could be no difficulty in ascertaining with respect to a person in this kingdom whether he was the servant of A. B. or not; but a captain of an English man of war, engaged in foreign service, has not the same means of satisfying himself upon such a fact. It might have been wholly inconsistent with the duties which he had to perform, in his character of a servant of the public, either to leave his ship, in order to make such enquiry himself, or to dispatch persons in that public service to enquire whether these slaves belonged to the. plaintiff or not. Supposing, during the absence of any of the persons detached on such duty, an occurrence had happened which required the exertions of the whole crew, it would have been no excuse to the Government of this country for him to say that he had detached some of his crew to ascertain whether certain persons who had come to his ship, and had been claimed as slaves by several persons residing in different places, in fact belonged to them. It might happen that every one of the slaves came from different places, and belonged to different owners, and it would have been necessary to make enquiries at each place. In this case the ship was within one mile of the shore, but it might have been fifty miles off. I am of opinion that the defendants were bound to act bona fide. If it could be made out that they acted mala fide, they would be liable to an action. But in order to support an action against a person who fills a public office like that

(a) 6 TR. 221.

which the defendants in this case filled, it is essential to show that
they acted mala fide. In this case the plaintiff claims the slaves as
his own, and desires that they should be dismissed from the defendant's ship and put into his possession. Sir G. Cockburn said that
they might go if the plaintiff could persuade them to go; but they
refused to go. It is said that Sir G. Cockburn ought to have
sent them away from his ship, but to what place was he to
send them ? They would refuse to go to East Florida, and
if he was bound to give them a boat, they would have the
option of going where they thought fit, and probably would have
gone to Cumberland Island; but the plaintiff desired to have
them put in his possession, no to have them set at large. Sir
G. Cockburn was called upon to consider a nice question of law,
upon which legal men might entertain a difference of opinion, viz.,
whether a man who is a slave in a country where slavery is tolerated,
continues a slave when he gets out of the limits of that state, and
whether neutrals are warranted in treating him as such. It appears
to me that Sir G. Cockburn acted *bona fide*. If he had said "these
men shall not remain longer in my ship, but I will put them into your
possession; they shall go where they will," it is clear that they would
not have gone back into the plaintiff's service. Instead of that,
however, Sir G. Cockburn writes to Sir A. Cochrane for instructions,
and the latter considers it a question fit to be decided upon by the
Government, and directs that the slaves should be conveyed to a
place of security, where they might be forthcoming for the benefit
of the plaintiff, if the Government should decide that they should
be restored to him. It appears to me, therefore, that the character
of *mala* fides does not attach upon either of the defendants in this
case, and that being so, I am of opinion that they did not, in the
language of this declaration, wrongfully harbour, detain, and keep
the slaves. Their character, as public officers, placed them in a
different situation from that in which other individuals would stand,
and, upon that ground, I am of opinion that the plaintiff is not
entitled to maintain this action.

HOLROYD, J. I am also of opinion that the plaintiff is not
entitled to maintain the present action. The declaration alleges that
the plaintiff was the proprietor, and in the possession of a cotton
plantation lying contiguous to the river St. John, in East Florida, on
which land he employed divers persons, his slaves, or servants. The
plaintiff, therefore, claims a general property in them as his slaves
or servants, and he claims this property, as founded, not upon any
municipal law of the country where he resides, but upon a general

right. This action is, therefore, founded upon an injury done to that general right. Now it appears, from the facts of the case, that the plaintiff had no right in these persons, except in their character of slaves, for they have were not serving him under any contract; and according to the principles of the English law, such a right cannot be considered as warranted by the general law of nature. I do not mean to say that particular circumstances may not introduce a legal relation to that extent, but assuming that there may be such a relation, it can only have a local existence, where it is tolerated by the particular ·law of the place, to which all persons there resident are bound to submit. Now if the plaintiff cannot maintain this action under the general law of nature, independently of any positive institution, then his right of action can be founded only upon some right which he has acquired by the law of the country where he is domiciled. If he, being a British subject could show that the defendant, also a British subject, had entered the country where he, the plaintiff was domiciled, and had done any act amounting to violation of that right, to the possession of slaves which was allowed by the laws of that country, I am by no means inclined to say that an action might not be maintained against him. The laws of England will protect the rights of British subjects, and give a remedy for a grievance committed by one British subject upon another; in whatever country that may be done. That, however, is a very different case from the present. Here, the plaintiff, a British subject, was resident in a Spanish colony, and perhaps it may be inferred, from what is stated in the special case, that, by the law of that colony slavery was tolerated. I am of opinion, that according to the principles of the English law, the right to slaves, even in a country where such rights are recognised by law, must be considered as founded not upon the law of nature, but upon the particular law of that country. And, supposing that the law of England would give a remedy for the violation of such a right, by one British subject to another (both being resident in, and bound to obey the laws of that country), still the right to these slaves being founded upon the law of Spain, as applicable to the Floridas, must be co-extensive with the territories of that State. I do not mean to say, that if the plaintiff having the right to possess these persons as his slaves there, had taken them into another place, where, by law, slavery also prevailed, his right would not have continued in such a place—the laws of both countries allowing a property in slaves. The law of slavery is, however, a law in *invitum*, and when a party gets out of

the territory where it prevails, and out of the power of his master,
and gets under the protection of another power, without any wrongful act done by the party giving that protection, the right of the
master, which is founded on the municipal law of the particular
place only, does not continue, and there is no right of action against
a party who merely receives the slaves in that country, without
doing any wrongful act. This has been decided to be the law with
respect to a person who has been a slave in any of our West India
colonies, and comes to this country. The moment he puts his foot
on the shores of this country, his slavery is at an end. Put the case
of an uninhabited island discovered and colonized by the subjects of
this country: the inhabitants would be protected and governed by
the laws of this country. In the case of a conquered country,
indeed, the old laws would prevail, until altered by the King in
Council; but in the case of the newly discovered country, freedom
would be as much the inheritance of the inhabitants and their
children, as if they were treading on the soil of England. Now,
suppose a person who had been a slave in one of our own West
India settlements, escaped to such a country, he would thereby
become as much a freeman as if he had come into England. He ceases
to be a slave in England only because there is no law which sanctions
his detention in slavery; for the same reason, he would cease to be a
slave the moment he landed in the supposed newly discovered island.
In this case, indeed, the fugitives did not escape to any island belonging to England, but they went on board an English ship (which for
this purpose may be considered a floating island), and in that ship
they became subject to the English laws above. They there stood
in the same situation in this respect as if they had come to an island
colonized by the English. It was not a wrongful act in the
defendants to receive them, quite the contrary. The moment they
got on board the English ship there was an end of any right which
the plaintiff had by the Spanish laws acquired over them as slaves.
They had got beyond the control of their master, and beyond the
territory where the law, recognising them as slaves, prevailed. They
were under the protection of another power. The defendants were
not subject to the Spanish law, for they had never entered the
Spanish territories either as friends or enemies. The plaintiff was
permitted to see the men, and to endeavour to persuade them to
return; but in that he failed. He never applied to be permitted to
use force; and it does not appear he had the means of doing so. I
think that Sir G. Cockburn was not bound to do more than he did;
whether he was bound to do so much it is unnecessary for me to

say. It was not a wrongful act in him, a British officer, to abstain from using force to compel the men to return to slavery. It does not appear that he prevented force being used. I do not say that he might not have refused, but in fact there was no refusal. I have given my opinion upon this question, supposing that there would be a right of action against these defendants, if a wrong had actually been done by them, but I am by no means clear, that even under such circumstances, any action would have been maintainable against them by reason of their particular situation as officers acting in discharge of a public duty, in a place *flagrante bello.* I doubt whether the application ought not to have been made in such a case to the governing powers of this country for redress. The cases from the Admiralty Courts are distinguishable from the present upon the grounds already stated by my Brother Bayley. In Madrazzo v. Willes, the plaintiff was a Spanish subject, and by the law of Spain slavery and the trade in slaves being tolerated, he had a right, by the laws of his own country, to exercise that trade. The taking away the slaves was an active wrong done in aggression upon rights given by the Spanish law. That is very different from requiring as in this case, an act to be done against the slaves, who had voluntarily left their master. When they got out of the ter ritory where they became slaves to the plaintiff, and out of his power and control, they were, by the general law of nature, made free, unless they were slaves by the particular law of the place where the defendant received them. They were not slaves by the law which prevailed on board the British ship of war. I am, therefore, of opinion that the defendants are entitled to the judgment of the Court.

BEST, J. The feelings which are naturally excited by a discussion of the subject of slavery may perhaps betray one into some warmth of expression ; I beg, however, that nothing which I say may be considered as trenching upon the local rights of the proprietors of lands in our West India islands to the services of their slaves in that country. They have acquired those rights under the encouragement of the legislature of this country, and they ought not to be put in jeopardy by any power in this country, unless a complete compensation be given to men by the public for the capital which they have been encouraged to embark in such property. The crime of slavery is the crime of the nations, and every individual in the nation should contribute to put an end to it as soon as possible. It is a relation which ought not to be continued one moment longer than is necessary to fit the slave for a state of freedom. For our

convenience or our gain it ought not to be allowed to exist. The
plaintiff in this case, states his rights in terms so general, that
possibly the declaration might have been bad upon demurrer, although
it is sufficiently certain after verdict. It is incumbent upon us,
however, to see what sort of servants the plaintiff claims. It is
clear, from the case, that they were not servants in one sense of the
word: that they were not servants by contract, but slaves. The
first objection that occurs to me in this case is, that it does not
appear upon the special case, that the right to slaves exists in East
Florida. That right is not a general, but a local right; it ought,
therefore, to have been shown that it existed in Florida, and that
the defendants knew of its existence. Assuming, however, that
those facts did appear, still, under the circumstances of this case,
this action could not be maintained. These slaves were not seduced
from the service of their employer by any act of the defendant; if
they had, the case would have been very different. The plaintiff,
therefore, can only be entitled to recover upon the count
which charges the defendants with harbouring the slaves. Then
the question is, were these persons slaves at the time when Sir G.
Cockburn refused to do the act which he was desired to do?
I am decidedly of opinion that they were then no longer slaves. The
moment they put their feet on board of a British man-of-war, not
lying within the waters of East Florida (there, undoubtedly, the
laws of that country would prevail), those persons who before had
been slaves, were free. The defendants were not guilty of any act
prejudicial to the rights which the plaintiff alleges to have been
infringed. Those rights were at an end before the defendants were
called upon to act. Slavery is a local law, and therefore, if a man
wishes to preserve his slaves, let him attach them to him by affection,
or make fast the bars of their prison, or rivet well their chains, for
the instant they get beyond the limits where slavery is recognised
by the local law, they have broken their chains, they have escaped
from their prison, and are free. These men, when on board an
English ship had all the rights belonging to Englishmen, and were
subject to all their liabilities. If they had committed any offence
they must have been tried according to English laws. If any
injury had been done to them they would have had a remedy by
applying to the laws of this country for redress. I think that Sir
G. Cockburn did all that he lawfully could do to assist the plaintiff:
he permitted him to endeavour to persuade the slaves to return, but
he refused to apply force. I think that he might have gone further,
and have said that force should not be used by others; for if any

force had been used by the master or any person in his assistance,
can it be doubted that these slaves might have brought an action of
trespass against the persons using that force? Nay, if the slave,
acting upon his newly recovered right of freedom, had determined to
vindicate that right originally the gift of nature, and had resisted
the force, and his death had ensued in the course of such resistance,
can there be any doubt that everyone who had contributed to that
death would, according to our laws, be guilty of murder? That is
substantially decided by Sommersett's case, from which, it is clear,
that such would have been the consequence had those slaves been in
England; for are not those on board an English ship as much protected and governed by the English laws as if they stood on English
land? If there be no difference in this respect Sommersett's case
has decided the present: he was held to be entitled to his discharge, and consequently, all persons attempting to force him back
into slavery would have been trespassers, and if death had ensued in
using that force would have guilty of murder. It has been said,
that Sir G. Cockburn might have sent them back. He certainly was
not bound to receive them into his own ship in the first instance,
but having done so, he would no more have forced them back into
slavery than he would have committed them to the deep. There
may possibly be a distinction between the situation of these persons
and that of slaves coming from our own islands, for we have unfortunately recognised the existence of slavery there, although we have
never recognised it in our own country. The plaintiff does not
found his action upon any violation of the English laws, but he relies
upon the comity of nations. I am of opinion, however, that he
cannot maintain any action in this country by the comity of nations.
Although the English law has recognised slavery, it has done so within
certain limits only; and I deny that in any case an action has been held
to be maintainable in the municipal courts of this country, founded
upon a right arising out of slavery. Let us look to the history of
the odious traffic out of which the relation of master and slave
in the West Indies has arisen. Queen Elizabeth expressed her hope
to Sir John Hawkins, that the negroes went voluntarily from Africa
to submit to domestic slavery in another country, and declared that
if any force was used to enslave them, she doubts not it would bring
down the rage of heaven upon those who were guilty of such
wickedness. It is unfortunate, however, for the memory of that
queen, that in her reign patents were granted to encourage the trade,
and those were followed up by Acts of Parliament expresssly
recognising it. The legislature interfering from motives of humanity,

regulated the mode of transporting slaves, and also the making of insurances upon them. An Act was also passed soon after we had accomplished our own liberty: viz., the 9 and 10, W. 3, c. 26, s. 7, 8, 9, which certainly speaks of these unhappy beings by the degrading appellations of merchandize and of their being brought to England, not as the termination of the voyage, but as a place at which ships might call. I think, however, that notwithstanding that act, if they had come here and got within the waters of England, they might have been discharged by means of writ of habeas corpus. There was also a statute passed in the reign of G. 2., (a) by which slaves in the West India islands, like other property, were made saleable, and subject to the debts of the persons to whom they belong. Both these statutes, however, were local in there application, being confined to the West India islands only. I do not, therefore, feel myself fettered by anything expressed in either of them, in pronouncing the same opinion upon the rights growing out of slavery, as if they had never passed. If, indeed, there had been any express law, commanding us to recognise those rights, we might then have been called upon to consider the propriety of that which has been said by the great commentator upon the laws of this country, "that if any human law should allow or enjoin us to commit an offence against the divine law, we are bound to transgress that human law." There is no statute recognising slavery which operates in the part of the British empire in which we are now called upon to administer justice. It is a relation that has always in British courts been held inconsistent with the constitution of the country. It is matter of pride to me to recollect that, whilst economists and politicians were recommending to the legislature the protection of this traffic, and senators were framing statutes for its promotion, and declaring it a benefit to the country, the judges of the land, above the age in which they lived, standing upon the high ground of natural rights, and disdaining to bend to the lower doctrine of expediency, declared that slavery was inconsistent with the genius of the English constitution, and that human beings could not be the subject matter of property. As a lawyer, I speak of that early determination, when a different doctrine was prevailing in the senate, with a considerable degree of professional pride.

I say there is not any decided case in which the power to maintain an action arising out of the relation of master and slave has been recognised in this country. I am aware of the case in

---

(a) 5 Geo. II., c 7, s 4.

Levinz, but there the question was never decided, and if it had, in the case of Smith v. Gould, the whole Court declared that the opinion there expressed is not law. And the same had before been said by Lord Holt in the case of Chamberlain v. Harvey (a). The case of Smith v. Brown and Cooper has been misunderstood. It has been supposed to establish the position, that an action may be maintained here for the price of a negro, provided the sale took place in a country where negroes were saleable by law. But that point was not decided. The Court only held that the question could not be agitated unless that fact was averred on the face of the declaration. In this case the slaves belonged to the subject of a foreign State. The plaintiff, therefore, must recover here upon what is called the comitas inter communitates; but it is a maxim that that cannot prevail in any case where it violates the law of our own country, the law of nature, or the law of our God The proceedings in our courts are founded upon the law of England, and that law is again founded upon the law of nature and the revealed law of God If the right sought to be enforced is inconsistent with either of these, the English Municipal courts cannot recognise it. I take it, that the principle is acknowledged by the laws of all Europe. It appears to have been recognised by the French courts in the celebrated case alluded to by Mr. Hargrave in his argument in Sommersett's case. Mr. Justice Blackstone in his commentaries vol. 1., p. 421 says—"Upon the law of nature and the law of revelation, depend all human laws; that is to say, no human law should be suffered to contradict these." Now if it can be shewn that slavery is against the law of nature and the law of God, it cannot be recognised in our courts. In vol. 1. p. 424, the same writer says, "the law of England abhors, and will not endure, the existence of slavery within this nation," and he afterwards says, that "a slave or negro the instant he lands in England, becomes a free man; that is, the will protect him in the enjoyment of his person and his property. Yet, with regard to any right which the master may have lawfully acquired to the perpetual service of John or Thomas, this will remain exactly in the same state as before;" and then, after some other observations which it is unnecessary to notice, he says, "whatever service the heathen negro owes of right to his master, by general, not by local law, the same (whatever it be) is he bound to render when brought to England and made a Christian." Whatever service he owed by the local law is got rid of the moment he got out of the local

---

(a) 1 Ld. Raymond, 146.

limits. Now what service can we owe to the general law? Service
to our country, service to our relations for the protection they have
afforded us, a service by compact. A state of slavery excludes all
possibility of a right to service arising by either of these means. A
slave has no country, he is not reared by or for his parents, or by his
parents, or for his own benefit, but for that of his master, he is capable
of compact. We have the authority of the civil law for saying that
slavery is against the rights of nature, Just. Lib. 1. tit. 3., s. 2. The
legislature of this country has given judgment upon the questions.
They have abolished the trade in slaves, they have even brought up,
at a great price, the rights of other countries to carry it on. We
might, perhaps, have called upon them to abandon the traffic without
remuneration. It might have been glorious thus to put down an
usurpation against the rights of nature ; but we had partici-
pated too largely in the iniquitous traffic to be justified in
throwing the first stone, and may be considered as having paid this
service as a sin-offering for our transgressions. In Sommersett's case
Lord Mansfield observes, "The difficulty of adopting the relation
without adopting it in all its consequences is indeed extreme, and
yet many of those consequences are absolutely contrary to the
municipal law of England. We have no authority to regulate the
conditions in which law shall operate." Sommersett was discharged. He might then have maintained an action against those
who had detained him, and if that be so, how can any action be
maintained against those defendants for not assisting in the detention
of those men? The place where the transaction took place was,
with respect to this question, the same as the soil of England. Had
the defendants detained these men on board their ships, near the
coast of England, a writ of habeas corpus would have set them
at liberty. How then can an action be maintained against those
gallant officers for doing that of their own accord which, by process
of law and a British court of justice, they might have been co mpelled
to do? I have before adverted to the narrower ground upon which
this case might have been decided, but if slavery be recognised by
any law prevailing in East Florida, the operation of that law is
local. It is an anti-Christian law, and one which violates the rights
of nature, and therefore ought not to be recognised here. For these
reasons I am of opinion, that our judgment must be for the defendants.

Judgment for the defendants.

APPENDIX.

COPY OF THE FUGITIVE SLAVE CIRCULAR OF JULY, 1875.—(SINCE REVOKED.)

My Lords Commissioners of the Admiralty are pleased to issue the following instructions with reference to the question how far officers in command of her Majesty's ships are justified in receiving on board fugitive slaves, who, escaping from their masters, may claim the protection of the British flag. 1. Cases of this class may be divided into three classes : —1. Where slaves come on board a ship or boat in harbour, or within territorial waters, either to escape from the alleged cruelty of their masters, or to avoid the consequences of their misdeeds. 2. Where the British ship or boat is on the high seas, and the refugee slave, escaping, perhaps, from a vessel also at sea, would be in danger of losing his life were he not received on board. 3. Where a person has been detained on shore in a state of slavery, and, escaping to a British ship or boat, claims British protection on the ground that he has been so detained contrary to treaties existing between Great Britain and the country from the shores of which he escapes, as in the case of territories which, like Oman, Madagascar, and Johanna, are partially free.

2. The broad rule to be observed is, that a fugitive slave should not be permanently received on board any description of ship under the British flag, unless his life would be endangered if he were not allowed to come on board. The reason for this rule is that, were it otherwise, the practical result would be, in the first instance. to encourage and assist a breach of the law of the country, and, next, to protect the person breaking that law. And a contrary rule would lead to endless disputes and difficulties with the legal masters of slaves; for it might happen, to take an extreme instance, that the whole slave portion of the crews of vessels engaged in the pearl fishery in the Persian Gulf, might take refuge on board British ships, and, if free there, their masters would be entirely ruined, and the mistrust and hatred caused in their minds would be greatly prejudicial to British interests.

3. Such being the general and broad rule, it remains to apply it as far as possible, to the three classes of cases mentioned above. In the first class, the slave must not be allowed to remain on board after it has been proved to the satisfaction of the officer in command that he is legally a slave. In the second, the slave should be retained on board on the ground that on the high seas the British vessel is a part of the dominions of the Queen, but when the vessel returns within the territorial limits of the country from a vessel of which the slave has escaped, he will be liable to be surrendered on demand being made, supported by necessary proofs. In the third class, a negro might claim protection on the ground that, being by the terms of a treaty free, he was, nevertheless, being detained as a slave. It would then become the duty of the commanding officer to satisfy himself as to the truth of this statement, and to be guided in his subsequent pro-

ceeding in regard to such person by the result of his inquiries. and the law which would then affect the case. Those interested in maintaining the slavery of the person claiming his freedom should assist at the inquiry, and, in the event of his claim being established, the local authorities should be requested to take steps to ensure his not relapsing into slavery.

4. As a general principle, care should be taken that slaves are not misled into the belief that they will find their liberty by getting under the British flag afloat, or induced by the presence of a British ship to leave their own ships, if at sea, or their employment if on shore.

5. When surrendering fugitive slaves, commanding officers should exercise their discretion in endeavouring, according to the circumstances of each case, to obtain an assurance that the slaves will not be treated with undue severity .

6. A special report is to be made of every case of a fugitive slave seeking refuge on board one of her Majesty's ships.

7. The above instructions are also to be considered part of the general slave trade instructions, and to be inserted at page 29 of that volume, with a heading of receipt of fugitive slaves.

By Command of their Lordships,

ROBERT HALL.

THE NEW CIRCULAR OF DECEMBER, 1875.

When any person professing or appearing to be a fugitive slave, seeks admission to your ship on the high sea, beyond the limit of territorial waters, and claims the protection of the British flag, you will bear in mind that Her Majesty's ships are not intended for the reception of persons other than their officers and crew. You will satisfy yourself, therefore, before receiving the fugitive on board, that there is some sufficient ground in the particular case for thus receiving him.

In any case, in which for reasons which you deem adequate, you have received a fugitive slave into your ship, and taken him under the protection of the British flag upon the high seas, beyond the limit of territorial waters, you should retain him in your ship if he desires to remain, until you have landed him in some country, or transferred him to some other ship, where his liberty will be recognised and respected.

Within the territorial waters of a foreign State, you are bound by the comity of nations, while maintaining the proper exemption of your ship from local jurisdiction, not to allow her to become a shelter for those who would be chargeable with a violation of the law of the place. If therefore, while your ship is within the territorial waters of a State where slavery exists, a person professing to be a fugitive slave seeks admission into your ship, you will not admit him unless his life would be in manifest danger if he were not received on board. Should you, in order to save him from this danger, receive him, you ought not, after the danger is past, to permit him to continue on board, but you will not entertain any demand for his surrender, or enter into any examination as to his status.

If, while your ship is in the territorial waters of any chief or State in Arabia or on the shores of the Persian Gulf, or on the East Coast of Africa, or in any island lying off Arabia or off such coast or shores, including Zanzibar, Madagascar, and the Comoro Islands, any person should claim admission to your ship and protection, on the ground that he has been kept in a state of slavery, contrary to treaties existing between Great Britain and the territory, you may receive him until the truth of his statement is examined into. In making this examination it is desirable that you should communicate with the nearest British consular authority; and you should be guided in your subsequent proceedings by the result of the examination.

In any case of doubt or difficulty you should apply for further instructions either to the senior officer of your division or the commander-in-chief, who will, if necessary, refer to the Admiralty.

A special report is to be made of every case of a fugitive slave seeking refuge on board your ship.

Note on our Recent Legislation for Suppressing the Slave Trade.

The Slave Trade (Consolidation) Act, 1873, 36 and 37 Vic. c. 88.

Passed 5th August, 1873.

Recites the Acts mentioned in its second schedule for carrying into effect treaties for suppressing the slave trade, and the expediency of consolidating same.

In Section 2—interpretation clause—amongst other definitions, it is enacted that "Foreign state includes any foreign nation, people, tribe, sovereign prince, chief, or headman."

Section 3 contains directions as to visitation, and seizure by cruizers of suspected slave vessels, as they may be either British, or belonging to a foreign state, in pursuance of any treaty with that state, with directions as to detention of vessels seized.

Section 4 enacts that vessels equipped for traffic as defined in 1st Schedule to the Act, are to be deemed engaged in the slave trade. "Provided that this Section shall not extend to the vessel of any foreign state, except so far as may be consistent with the treaty made with such state."

Sections 5, 6, 7, 8, contains provisions as to Courts and their jurisdiction: proceedings on seizure by a foreigner, mixed Courts, and their powers.

Sections 9 and 10 relate to the disposal of condemned vessels, and slaves found on board.

Sections 11 to 16 relate to payment of bounties to captors—British or foreign—and the following important clauses bearing on the responsibilities, and indemnity of our naval officers.—

"When any visitation, seizure, detention, or prosecution purports to have been made and instituted in pursuance of this Act, the Treasury when required under any treaty shall and in any other case may, if they think fit, pay the whole or any part of any costs, expenses, compensation, and damage which may have been awarded against the person making or instituting such visitation, seizure, detention, or prosecution, or any costs and expenses which may have been incurred in respect of the same, or on account of any person on board any vessel so visited, seized, or detained ; but nothing in this Section shall exempt the commander or officer of the ship or other person by whom the visitation, seizure, detention, or prosecution was made or instituted from his liability to make good any sum so paid when required by the Treasury so to do, and when any such commander or officer, or other person serving under the Admiralty, or any person serving under any other Department of the Government, is so required to make good any sum, that sum shall, if the Treasury so direct, be deducted by the Admiralty or other Department of the Government, under whom such person is serving, from any payment to which such commander, officer, or person is entitled on account of salary, pay, prize, or bounty."

Section 17 to 23 contain miscellaneous provisions, 17 providing—

" All persons authorised to make seizures under this Act shall, in making and prosecuting any such seizure, have the benefit of all the protection granted to persons authorised to make seizures under any Act for the time being in force relating to Her Majesty's Customs in the United Kingdom, in like manner as if the enactments granting such protection were herein enacted, and in terms made applicable thereto."

Section 24 provides that—

" This Act shall be construed as one with the enactments of the Slave Trade Act, 1824, and any enactments amending the same, so far as they are in force at the time of the passing of this Act, and are not repealed by this Act ; and the expression 'this Act,' when used in this Act, shall include those enactments."

Section 25 to 29 contains miscellaneous provisions.

Section 30 repeals the acts specified in the second schedule.

THE FIRST SCHEDULE,

Contains an enumeration of equipments which are to be prima facie evidence of a vessel being engaged in the slave trade.

THE SECOND SCHEDULE

Acts repealed, viz :—

59 Geo. 3, c. 16 ; 7 & 8 Geo. 4, c. 54 ; 7 & 8 Geo. 4, c 74 ; 11 Geo. 4 & 1 Wm. 4, c 55 ; 3 & 4 Wm. 4, c 72 ; 5 & 6 Wm. 4, c 60, 61 ; 6 & 7 Wm. 4, c 6 81 ; 7 Wm. 4 & 1 Vic., c 62 ; 1 & 2 Vic., c 39, 40, 41, 47, 83, 84, & 102 ; 2 & 3 Vic., c 73 ; 3 & 4 Vic., c. 64, 67, 40, 41, 42, 59, 91, 101, 114 ; 6 & 7 Vic., c 14, 15, 16, 46, 50, 51, 52, 53 ; 7 & 8 Vic., c 26 ; 11 & 12 Vic., c 116 & 128 ; 12 & 13 Vic., c 84 ; 16 & 17 Vic., c 16 & 17 ; 18 & 19 Vic,, c 85 ; 25 & 26 Vic., c 40 ; 26 & 27 Vic., c 34 ; 32 & 33 Vic., c 2.—The whole of these.

5 Geo. 4, c 113.—The whole act, except sections 2 to 11, section 12 down to " taken to be in full force," sections 39, 40, & 47 ; 6 & 7 Vic., c 98, section 3 ; 16 & 17 Vic., c 107, section 189.

The Slave Trade, East African Coasts, 36 and 37 Vic., c. 59.

Passed 5th Aug., 1873.

"An act for regulating and extending the Jurisdiction in matters connected with the Slave Trade of the Vice-Admiralty Court at Aden, and of Her Majesty's Consul under Treaties with the Sovereigns of Zanzibar, Muscat, and Madagascar, and under future Treaties."

This act is only here noticed as containing a provision as to jurisdiction of the East African Courts .—"When the vessel seized s not shown to be entitled to claim the protection of the flag of *any* foreign state,"—a case which the Slave Trade Consolidation Act does not seem to allude to, and the practice as to which does not seem to be very clearly established.

NOTE ON RIGHT OF SEARCHING SLAVE VESSELS.

As the result of a correspondence extending over some years, in which Lords Palmerston, Aberdeen, Malmesbury, Clarendon, Derby, Brougham, and Carlisle, took part, Mr. Dana sums up as follows :—
" The principle, however, is clear. If a cruiser stops a vessel in the exercise of police power, he takes the chance of her turning out to be subject to the exercise of that power by him. If she prove to be a vessel of his own nation, or of one that has conceded to him that right, he turns out to have been in the exercise of a right *ab initio;* and neither he nor his nation is bound to make apology or compensation, though he vessel proves innocent of the crime suspected. But, if the vessel proves not to be subject to his police power, then he turns out to have been a trespasser *ab initio*, whether the vessel proves innocent or guilty of the crime suspected. He is liable in that case, not for having stopped an innocent vessel, but for having stopped one not subject to his inspection.

The mistake of the cruiser, however natural or honest, is not a justification. It is only an excuse, addressing itself to the consideration of the government whose vessel he has interfered with."—WHEATON, 8th Ed. (1866) by Dana, s. 135, p, 216.

HORACE EDWARDS, PRINTER, CHELTENHAM

Printed in the United States
By Bookmasters